A Status of Adivasis/Indigenous Peoples Land Series – 4

JHARKHAND

Alex Ekka

A Status of Adivasis/Indigenous Peoples Land Series – 4 : JHARKHAND
Alex Ekka

First Published, 2011
Reprinted 2020

ISBN 978-93-5002-150-7

Published by
AAKAR BOOKS
28 E Pocket IV, Mayur Vihar Phase I, Delhi 110 091
Phone : 011 2279 5505 Telefax : 011 2279 5641
aakarbooks@gmail.com; www.aakarbooks.com

In association with
THE OTHER MEDIA
C 44, IInd Floor, Housing Society
South Extension Part I, New Delhi 110 049
Phones : 011 2462 9372/73 Fax : 011 4104 2271
Email : tom@theothermedia.org

Printed at
Sapra Brothers, Noida.

Acknowledgements

The Status Report of Adivasis/Indigenous Peoples (SAIP) has been an important initiative of The Other Media and All India Coordinating Forum of Adivasis/Indigenous Peoples. It began with a lot of interest and enthusiasm with a wide consultation among activists, scholars and researchers interested in the Adivasis/Indigenous People's issues. However, the process seemed to have had its own pace and could not keep up with the expectation of completing the report on time. The present phase of the programme has covered, state-wise, issues of land and mining in the Adivasis/Indigenous People's areas.

This report on land issues in the Adivasi areas of Jharkhand has been prepared by Alex Ekka. We gratefully acknowledge the efforts made by the authors and members of the Editorial Collective (EC) in preparing this report.

Members of the EC went through the reports and gave their valuable comments and suggestions on the report. We gratefully acknowledge their contribution that was available at every stage of preparation of the report. The efforts of the EC have been untiringly coordinated by C R Bijoy. The reports owe a lot to his relentless efforts to keep in the loop everyone concerned towards producing good results out of the reports. At the level of The Other Media, Ravi Hemadri, who worked as the Executive Director of the organisation through most part of the programme served as a link between the organisation and the EC. He continued to coordinate the final editing and printing of the reports. We gratefully acknowledge the role played by both C R Bijoy and Ravi Hemadri.

We acknowledge and thank the Adivasi Academy, Tejgarh, Gujarat, and particularly Prof Ganesh Devy, for generously hosting in February, 2008, a two-day workshop of members of the EC and authors to review the draft reports. We thank the members of the Advisory Board of the SAIP, who with their participation in the first consultation and later whenever called upon, gave their inputs to the reports. Thanks are due to Shankar Gopalakrishnan who meticulously put together statistical data and selected literature for SAIP.

Finally we would like to acknowledge and thank our funders ICCO, Netherlands, and TROCAIRE, Ireland, who supported the programme right through the last five years. We are grateful to the Foundation for Ecological Security, Anand, Gujarat, who generously supported the printing of the first phase of reports on land. We thank all of them for being patient with this initiative.

December, 2010

E Deenadayalan
General Secretary

Contents

Preface

Eighty-eight million Adivasis and indigenous peoples live in India—approximately one fourth of the world's total indigenous population. Historically self-sufficient, forest-based communities with independent cultural identities, they have been subjected to displacement, dispossession and repression for more than a century and are now India's poorest and most marginalised communities. Since the onset of British rule, and in many cases from much earlier, Adivasis and indigenous peoples have been systematically and forcibly dispossessed of the resources of their homelands. In gross violation of democratic practice, social justice and both constitutional and legal requirements, such dispossession continues to this day. It is also the Adivasis and indigenous peoples who have paid the heaviest price for the current neo-liberal globalisation policies, with their land, resources and forests taken from them for private capital - in the name of 'economic growth.'

These larger processes have been accompanied by the erosion and undermining of cultural identities, leading to a loss of cultural moorings and other markers of ethnicity. Less than half of India's Adivasi communities speak their own language. State and private efforts at 'mainstreaming' and against indigenous faiths, practices and cultural mores have had a devastating impact.

Such trends have not gone unchallenged. Despite growing differentiation, ethnicity has emerged as a strong, consolidating force. Many have organised, often with the help of sympathetic outsiders, to fight against their oppressors and struggle for the control over land and other resources, and for local self-government as in parts of Central India. There have been demands for political self-determination and autonomy of varying degrees as in Jharkhand and the north-east. The state characterises all such struggles as 'Law and Order Problems', and large parts of central India and the north-east are heavily militarised in the name of 'national security'. In other parts too state repression has been heavy and brutal.

Though these processes are well known to many and particularly to Adivasis and indigenous people's movements, there continues to be a dearth of knowledge on the overall status of Adivasis and indigenous peoples in India. The struggle-based mass organisations of Adivasis and indigenous peoples in the Indian subcontinent articulated the need to work towards such a task in the late 1990s. The collective process to fulfil this task was launched in 2005.

The Status of Adivasis/Indigenous Peoples is conceptualised as a series of reports on salient themes affecting the lives of Adivasis/Indigenous Peoples. In the first instance, the series focuses on the situation of land and mining in the tribal tracts of the country. We hope that the series will be effective in not only deliberating upon similar themes of importance to the Adivasi present and future, but also help strengthening linkages amongst movements, activists, scholars and all others who are concerned with the protection of the rights of Adivasis/Indigenous Peoples in the Indian subcontinent.

This series of reports will explore the history, the laws, and the facts, and describe struggles while providing an overview of current realities. The main purpose of these reports is to expand linkages and relationships between movements, scholars, and activists so that the future of the political struggles is informed and forward looking.

Executive Summary

The tribal people and their lands are inseparable just like fish and water. The lands and the resources not only give sustenance to the tribal people but also are the basis of their cultural identity as well as of their socio-political systems. In reciprocity these are harnessed and nurtured by the tribal people. On account of such symbiotic relationship both have survived, albeit at different levels. Today when the world is facing a great ecological and environmental crisis, we must learn from the tribal people as how to restore that symbiotic relationship.

This study on tribal lands in Jharkhand has been made at such a time when the tribal people are suffering the most on account of land alienation and when the ecological degradation is at its worst on account of the non-sustainable development process. This study is more pertinent as the state of Jharkhand is rich in natural resources but its people, especially the tribals and the indigenous people, are poor. The situation is more grim as the tribals constitute only 26.30 per cent of the total population of the state and the primitive tribes about 0.71 per cent with a dwindling population of 19, 2051 according to the 2001 census. Even the constitutional provisions of the Fifth Schedule covering 112 Community Development Blocks as Scheduled areas in the state have not prevented tribal land alienation and have not brought about significant overall development among the tribal people.

The three main legislations to prevent tribal alienation in Jharkhand are the Chotanagpur Tenancy Act, (CNTA) 1908, the Wilkinson's Rule (WR) 1837 and the Santal Parganas

Tenancy Act, (SPTA) 1949. The CNTA was meant to prevent the *Mundari Khutkatti* (original settlers of the Munda tribe) and the *Uraon Bhuinhari* (original settlers of the Uroan tribe). The Wilkinson's Rule was specially meant for the Ho tribals of Singhbhum with specific land tenure system under the *Munda – Manki* traditional system of governance. Similarly, the SPTA was meant to protect the lands of the Santals. But many amendments brought about in these legislations by the governments down the years have watered them down severely. As a result tribal land alienation continues unabated even today.

The customary tribal land inheritance systems among the tribals of Jharkhand are patrilineal in order to prevent the land alienation. However the widow and the unmarried daughters are given the maintenance land till the death of the former and the marriage of the latter. After the marriage of the daughters their lands are divided among their brothers. But if the daughter is the only surviving child in the family, she is entitled to her father's property till she gets married, after which it goes to the closest male agnates of her father.

A declining trend of landholding has been observed among the tribals. On an average the per capita landholding of tribals in the scheduled area declined from 0.71 ha during 1971 to 0.51 ha during 2001. The main reasons for the declining tribal landholding pattern are land fragmentation due to increase in population and land acquisition for development projects causing displacement of people.

Around the first millennium BC there was the community land ownership. But it changed into the state formation under the tribal chieftain Phani Mukut Rai in the 13th century. During the Mougal rule the tribal chieftain Durjan Sal gave lands to the non-tribal courtiers and officials as service grants. Thus began the *Jagirdari* system. Similarly, the *Zamindari* system started under the British with the introduction of the Permanent Settlement in 1773. This forcible land alienation led to a series of tribal revolts like the Tamar revolt of 1789, the Kol rebellion of 1819-20 and the Santal insurrection of

1856. The new direct administration was introduced by brining the Chotanagpur region covering an area of 32,500 sq. km under the South-West Frontier Agency in 1834. It embodied the concept of a non-regulation administrative system under a benign paternalistic agent, Captain Wilkinson. He also started the Wilkinson's Rule among the Hos of Singhbhum as mentioned above.

Then came the Regulation of XX of 1854, which abolished the South West Frontier Agency and Chotanagpur passed under the Lieutenant Governor of Bengal as a non-Regulation Province, which was administered by a Deputy Commissioner. This was done to prevent the robbing of tribal people through force and fraud by the foreign landlords. But the situation was no different under the Regulation of XX of 1854. And yet the Chotanagpur Tenures Act, 1869 was promulgated to quell the revolting tribal population and safeguard the interests of the landlords.

The Survey Settlement – also known as *Bhuinhari* Settlement – (1861-1880) further aggravated the tribal land alienation as it accepted the legal rights of the landlords, *thikkedars* and the moneylenders and the legal rights over the land forcibly grabbed from the original farmers. Its purpose was to legitimize the loot of these alien culprits.

The *Bhugut Bandha* was another legal measure of tribal land alienation. It was a kind of mortgage according to the Chotanagpur Tenures Act (Amendment) of 1903. It fixed the time limit to 7 years, so that at the end of that period the principal and the capital amount were extinguished. But this Act did not define the term *Bhuinhari* land, which gave rise to innumerable disputes and lawsuits. The Act presupposed that the ultimate owner of the village was the Maharaja.

The Mundas prayed to the Commissioner, the Lieutenant Governor and the Secretary of State in vain. They insisted on their rights to land and told how the foreign landlords had taken away their ancestral properties. But the Government found their petition to be unreasonable and extravagant, hence the appeals were rejected.

Jharkhand has had a history of tribal land alienation. As noted above it started during the Mougal Empire under the tribal chieftain Durjan Sal through the *Jagirdari* system and during the British through the *Zamindari* system. Further due to revenue collection from land and forests as the prime objective of the British colonial rule all tribal people's rebellions for land restoration were suppressed. Similarly, settled agriculture was forced upon the tribals and the shifting cultivation abandoned. Further in 1856 the colonial government disposed of the indigenous people of their forest through a government order and through the Indian Forest Act 1878. The post independence scenario is marked by a conspicuous paradox between the policies and functioning of the state with regard to the tribal interests in the country. Therefore despite the liberal ideology as reflected in the Indian Constitution, the bureaucracy and the judiciary hold a pragmatic view. The ruling classes and castes already politically powerful want to be also economically powerful and make money at the faster rate. The senseless exploitation of the natural wealth, both forest and minerals and the height of corruption in the administrative level on one hand and the bankruptcy of the public sector industries on the other prove the point.

In urban areas tribal land alienation has been primarily demand induced—for housing and non-agricultural purposes. In the rural areas the land alienation is basically to meet the day-today needs of cash starved poor Adivasis. In the absence of active land markets in rural areas, people resort to illegal mortgages and at times outright sales. The third type of land alienation is for the public purpose through the major, medium and small development projects like dams, industries, hydropower stations and mines to mention a few. This development induced displacement after independence has caused the land alienation of 30 lakh acres from 1951 till now. Tribal land alienation got aggravated in the era of globalization since 1991 in India. There are about 74 MOUs of the multinational companies to be signed by the Jharkhand government, which will but alienate thousands of acres of tribal lands in the state. Another frightening feature of tribal land alienation is through the fraudulent and forcible land grabbing of the tribal people by the non-tribals.

The scenario of tribal alienation has not changed but has aggravated today. Consequently the tribal people have resorted to movements to protect their lands and resources in the state and have been successful to some extent. The Koel Karo movement against the hydropower project was shelved by the Jharkhand Government after almost 40 years of people's resistance. Similarly, the people's non-violent movement against the Netarhat Field Firing Project in 1994 managed to halt the land acquisition for one decade. It has surfaced again as the government has served fresh notification for land acquisition for the proposed project. The project affected people are once again putting up a stiff resistance.

In the face of such a situation in the state this study is timely made on tribal land alienation. It is expected that it will strengthen the civil society and the people's organization to protect the tribal people's lands and their very identity.

Introduction

Jharkhand, meaning land of forests is well known for its rich mineral resources. It became the 28th State of India on 15 November 2000. The region has a history of Adivasi struggles against non-Adivasi incursion and domination, even as it is the case today. Though Jharkhand is the heartland of the Adivasis in Eastern India, they are a minority today facing economic deprivation through land alienation and political subjugation by non-Adivasis more than ever before, hence the significance of this study.

The study on Adivasi lands in Jharkhand has eight main sections. Section one gives a general background to the state in terms of the tribal population including the geographical location and the Scheduled Areas. It also describes briefly the primitive tribal groups in the state. Section two describes the land tenure systems in the state covering land types, ownership and inheritance patterns. Similarly, section three discusses the individual and communal land holding pattern according to the Adivasis in the state and section four gives a historical narrative of the process of the changing *adivasi*-land relationship. Adivasi land alienation is analyzed in section five, especially with regard to various survey settlements, forest laws, land acquisition for development projects, land reforms, other forms of tribal land alienation, protective legislations, urban development and tourism etc. Thereafter, section six spells out Adivasi women's land rights, particularly on their role in resource control, systems of property, inheritance rights and their struggles. Section seven examines the nature of land use pattern and types of crops grown, productivity and fragmentation of land, impact of commercial agriculture and status of shifting agriculture. And finally section eight gives an overall conclusion with some reflections and insights.

1

Background of the State

The total geographical area of Jharkhand is 79,714 sq. km or 7.97 million hectares, having the total cultivable area of 3.8 million hectares of which the net sown area is 1.804 million hectares (25% of the total area) and the net irrigated area is 1.57 million hectares (8% of the net sown area). It has a population of 26,945,829 according to the 2001 census, with 13,885,037 males and 13,060,792 females. The Scheduled Tribes population is 7,087,066, which is 26.3% of the total population in the state and the male and female tribal population is 3,565,960 and 3,521,108 respectively.

1.1 The Scheduled Tribes of Jharkhand

The Scheduled Castes and Scheduled Tribes Order (Amendment) Act, 1976 declares 30 tribes to be scheduled for the state of Jharkhand, including 9 primitive tribal groups. They are the Asur, the Baiga, the Banjara, the Bathudi, the Bedia, the Binjhia, the Birhor, the Bhumij the Chero, the Chick Baraik, the Gond, the Gorait, the Ho, the Karmali, the Kharia, the Kharwar, the Khond, the Kisan, the Kora, the Korwa, the Lohra, the Mahli, the Mal Paharia, the Munda, the Uraon, the Parhaiya, the Santhal, the Sauria Paharia, the Hill Kharia, and the Savar. The most numerous are the Santhals followed by the Uraons, Kharwars, Mundas and Kharias. The tribes of this region are of Austric and Dravidian stocks. The Mundas, the Hos, the Kharias etc. speak languages belonging to the Austro-Asiatic language family, whereas the Uraons and the Paharias speak Dravidian languages.

Table 1 : District-wise Scheduled Tribes Population in Jharkhand

S. N.	*Districts*	*Persons*		*Male*		*Female*	
		Total	*%*	*Total*	*%*	*Total*	*%*
1.	Garhwa	158,959	15.35	81,605	51.34	77,354	48.66
2.	Palamau	392,325	18.70	199,311	50.80	193,014	49.20
3	Latehar						
4.	Chatra	30,384	03.84	15,571	51.25	14,813	48.75
5.	Hazaribagh	268,333	11.78	136,409	50.84	131,924	49.16
6.	Ramgarh						
7.	Koderma	4,067	00.81	2,163	52.94	1,914	47.06
8.	Giridih	184,469	09.69	94,005	50.96	90,464	49.04
9.	Deoghar	142,717	12.25	72,780	51.00	69,937	49.00
10.	Godda	247,538	23.62	124,716	50.38	122,822	49.62
11.	Sahibganj	270,423	29.15	135,222	50.00	135,201	50.00
12.	Pakur	312,838	44.59	157,777	50.43	155,061	49.57
13.	Dumka	701,903	39.89	352,306	50.19	349,597	49.81
14.	Jamtara						
15.	Dhanbad	202,729	08.46	103,100	50.86	99,629	49.14
16.	Bokaro	218,600	12.30	112,184	51.32	106,416	48.68
17.	Ranchi	1,164,624	41.82	585,582	50.28	579,042	49.72
18	Khunti						
19.	Lohardaga	203,053	55.70	101,888	50.18	101,165	49.82
20.	Gumla	920,597	68.36	549243	49.89	461354	50.11
21	Simdega						
22.	W. Singhbhum	1,111,322	53.36	553903	49.84	557419	50.16
23.	Saraikela-Kharsawan						
24.	East Singhhum	552,187	27.85	278205	50.38	273982	49.62
	Jharkhand	7,087,068	26.30	3655970	50.32	3521108	49.68

Source: Census 2001

As six districts were created after 2000, the census figures in Table 1 of these districts are put along with their parent districts. These are Latehar, Ramgarh, Jamtara, Khunti,

Simdega and Saraikela-Kharsawan. The tribal population of Jharkhand is 26.30% of the total population of the state in 2001. It was 27.76% in 1991. This reveals a decreasing trend in the tribal population. The sex ratio of Jharkhand is 941, which is higher than the national average of 933 per 1000 male. In Adivasi communities, both boys and girls are equal and there is no bias against the girl child. The literacy rate among the tribals is 40.67% and, it is 53.98% for male and 27.21% and female respectively. Significantly the female tribal literacy rate in this state is much higher than those of other states. Much of the credit for this higher tribal literacy rate goes to the missionaries (Louis 2007:143).

1.2 The Primitive Tribal Groups

The Primitive Tribal Groups in Jharkhand are the Asur, the Birhor, the Birjia, the Korwa, the Hill Pahariya, the Paharia, the Savar and the Sauriya Pahariya. The total population of the primitive tribes in Jharkhand is 1,94,835[1] . Relatively more numerous are the Sauriya Paharia with a population of 61,121 followed by the Mal Paharia with a population of 60,756. The least numerous are the Hill Khariya with a population of 1554 and the Birhor with a population of 6579 only.[2]

These tribal groups are nomadic and still in the food gathering stage. They roam about in the forests for their livelihood. Because of their nomadic nature, literacy, healthcare and settled agriculture have been delayed to them. If these groups are not taken care of, they may entirely be wiped out. Practically all the primitive tribal groups have shown a negative population growth. This is due to low birth rate and high mortality, high infant mortality, susceptibility to diseases, low health status and threat from endemic diseases like sickle cell, anemia and infertility to mention a

1. According to a survey conducted by the Tribal Welfare Research Institute, Ranchi (2002-2003).
2. TRI. 2003. *Survey of the Primitive Tribal Groups in Jharkhand*. Ranchi: Tribal Research Institute.

Table 2: District-wise Primitive Tribes in Jharkhand

Districts	*Asur*	*Birhor*	*Birjiya*	*Korwa*	*Hill Khariya*	*Mal Paharia*	*Paharia*	*Sawar*	*Sauriya Pahariya*	*Total*
Bokaro	0	297	0	0	0	0	0	0	0	297
Chatra	0	1256	0	1322	0	0	0	0	0	2578
Deoghar	0	0	0	0	0	6341	74	0	0	6415
Dhanbad	0	137	0	0	0	0	0	0	0	137
Dumka	4	0	0	0	0	31546	0	0	0	31550
E.Singhbhum	0	58	0	0	1554	626	0	9182	320	11740
Garwha	0	159	0	18144	0	0	3264	0	0	21567
Giridhih	0	258	0	0	0	0	0	0	0	258
Godda	0	0	0	0	0	1451	0	27	14624	16102
Gumla	7700	141	1266	1914	0	0	134	0	0	11155
Hazaribagh	0	1873	0	0	0	0	0	0	0	1873
Jamtara	0	0	0	0	0	3339	0	0	0	3339
Kodarma	0	766	0	106	0	0	245	0	0	1117
Latehar	226	94	3731	1518	0	0	2945	0	0	8514
Lohardaga	1170	58	425	0	0	0	0	0	0	1653
Pakur	0	0	0	0	0	16902	0	0	10530	27432
Palamau	0	0	0	2126	0	100	5220	0	0	7446
Ranchi	0	636	0	0	0	9	0	0	107	752
Seraikela	0	87	0	0	0	0	0	695	853	1635
Sahibganj	0	0	0	0	0	442	0	0	34687	35129
Simdega	0	174	0	603	0	0	0	0	0	777
W.Singhbhum	0	585	0	0	0	0	0	0	0	585
PTG TOTAL	9100	6579	5422	25733	1554	60756	11882	9904	61121	192051

Source: Tribal Welfare Research Institute, Ranchi. Survey of the Primitive Tribal Groups in Jharkhand (2002-2003).

few. The literacy rate among the primitive tribes is less than 10% and among women it is as dismally poor as 2% to 3%. Interventions made through the Ashram Schools and the Model Residential Schools have had some impact on them, but due to their culture and life style, many students dropout from the school and the girl children are rarely sent to school.

1.3 The Scheduled Areas

The two historical divisions of Jharkhand are the Chotanagpur Plateau and the Santhal Parganas. The State is divided into five Administrative Divisions (North Chotanagpur, South Chotanagpur, Dumka, Palamau, and Kolhan) and 24 Districts. It is further divided into the Scheduled and the non-Scheduled Areas. The present

Table 3 : Scheduled Area Districts and Population in Jharkhand

S. N.	*Name of District*	*No. of Blocks*	*Total Population*	*ST Population*	*ST%*
1.	Ranchi (including Khunti District)	20	2,785,064	1,164,624	41.82
2.	Lohardaga	05	364,521	203,053	55.70
3.	Gumla (including Simdega District)	18	1,346,767	920,597	68.36
4.	West Singhbhum (including Saraikela-Kharsawan District)	23	2,082,795	1,111,322	53.36
5.	East Singhbhum	09	1,982,988	552,187	27.85
6.	Latehar	07	467,071	211,580	45.30
7.	Garhwa (Bhandaria Block)	01	43,020	26,047	60.55
8.	Dumka	14	1,759,602	701,903	41.37
9.	Sahibganj	07	736,835	228,990	33.08
10.	Pakur	06	701,664	312,838	44.59
11.	Godda (Barijor and Sundarpahari Blocks)	02	144,867	99,769	68.87
	Total	112	12,415,194	5,532,910	44.57

Source: Census 2001

Scheduled Areas as per the Order of 1977 are the Districts of Ranchi, Lohardaga, Gumla, Simdega, East Singhbhum, West Singhbhum, Jamtara, Pakur, Dumka, Sahibganj, (the 2003 Notification left out two blocks viz Mandro and Udhwa), Latehar District, (the 2003 Notification left out two Panchyats Rabda and Bokoria), Bhandaria Block of Garwa District, Sundar Pahari and Boarijor blocks of Godda District. To this were added the new Districts of Khunti and Simdega in 2007. The rest of the areas come under the non-Scheduled Areas. They are Hazarigagh, Palamau, Dhanbad, Bokaro, Koderma and the new District of Ramgarh. Ranchi is the capital of Jharkhand.

Jharkhand is the Adivasi heartland of Eastern India, having abundance of mineral resources. And yet, the Adivasis today are in a minority. The primitive tribal groups, though few, draw no less attention for their overall welfare and development. The newfound state of Jharkhand has not altered the exploitation of Adivasis, especially through land alienation despite 112 Blocks coming under the Scheduled Areas where the Scheduled Tribes population has come down substantially as compared to the previous census.

2

Tribal Land Tenures

The tribal land tenures today originate from three specific legislations - the Chotanagpur Tenancy Act (CNTA) 1908, the Wilkinson's Rule (WR) 1837 and the Santal Parganas Tenancy Act (SPTA) 1949. While the CNTA pertained mainly to the Mundas and Uraons of the old Ranchi district, the WR was specific to the Hos of Singhbhum and the SPTA was meant for the Santals of Santhal Parganas. The tribal land tenure system can thus be discussed in three main sections below. It will be followed by the inheritance pattern among Adivasis .

2.1 Tribal Land Tenure under CNTA

The CNTA was legislated in 1908 to stop tribal land alienation, chiefly the *khuntkatti* and the *bhuinhari* lands of the Mundas and the Uraons respectively. These lands belonged to the original Munda and Uroan settlers. The lands and forests within the village boundary were owned in common by the village community and could not be disposed off to outsiders without unanimous consent of all. Although at present a Munda of a *khuntkatti* village or an Uroan of a *bhuinhari* village are allowed to cultivate a specific portion of the land and on their death leave them to their respective heirs, the *khuntkati* and the *bhuinhari* brotherhoods still hold the power to redistribute the village lands if the need should arise.[3]

3. Ekka, P. 2003. *Tribal Movements: A Study in Social Change*, Pathalgaon: Tribal Research and Documentation Centre, p. 36.

2.1.1 Description of Tribal Land Tenure System

There are three major types of tribal land tenure systems as described briefly below:

i) Mundari *Khuntkattidar*

The descendants of the Munda founder of the village are called the Mundari *Khuntkattidars.* This Munda, along with his lineage brothers, owns the village including the land and the forest within its boundary. They do not pay tax, but rent for the land. According to the Settlement Report of 1927, there were 156 intact and 449 broken Mundari *Khuntkatti* villages in Ranchi district. In the intact villages, the land is under the control of the Mundas only whereas in the broken ones people who are not the descendants of the original founder, including non-tribal, have occupied land.

ii) *Bhuinhari* Tenure

These lands are in non-Mundari areas, which have been reclaimed and bought under cultivation by original claimants like Uraons of the village or their descendants. They enjoy the status of tenure-holders and hold land either rent free or at quit rent fixed in perpetuity. The total area of the *Bhuinhari* land according to the last settlement was 215 sq. miles.

iii) *Raiyats*

Raiyat means the owner and cultivator of the land. *Raiyats* are of two types: (1) *Raiyats* holding *khuntkatti* rights and (2) *Raiyats* not holding *khuntkatti* rights. The *Raiyats* holding *khuntkatti* rights reside in non-Mundari areas, excluding the villages covered by the *Bhuinhari* land. They are the descendants of the original village founders who had cleared the forests. Their number in *khuntkatti* tenancies recorded in the last survey was 938. The non-*khuntkatti* rights holding *raiyats* are other tribals and non-tribals. With the gradual breakdown of the tribal land system due to the invasion of the non-tribals in the region, the tribal tenures gradually disintegrated. In the process, some lands came in the hands of other tribals and non-tribal people. Presently, most holdings are coming under the *raiyats* of this category.

2.1.2 Tenancy Surveys prior to Independence

The main sources of land and community rights for the Adivasis are the *khatians* or record of rights, that were created during the initial and revisional survey and settlement carried out under the CNTA. They are in three parts: Part I is the '*Khewat*' or record of rights, which shows the order of rights in each plot of land; Part II is a record of 'Community Rights', also known as *Khatian* Part II, and Part III is the 'Village Note'. It describes the social and economic organization of each village, the rights and duties of headmen and community rights in land and resources.

In the two major surveys carried out in Ranchi district during the colonial period - in 1902-10 and a revisional survey in 1927-28 - two categories of community or non-private lands were recorded (apart from the Mundari *khuntkatti* land) uncultivated 'common lands' (*gair mazrua malik* or *khas*), and other community lands, that were put to specific uses, such as graveyards, sacred groves, village roads, etc. (*gair mazrua am*).

Uncultivated 'waste' and jungle land accounts for the largest amount of common land, and is referred to by the term *gair mazrua khas*. Although by custom such land was under the control of local communities, during the settlement, they were recorded in the '*gair muazua khatas*' of the superior tenure holders, such as the *zamindars* of each village or of the Mundari *khuntkattidars* in their areas. However, the specific rights of various groups, including the landlords, *khuntkattidars, raiyats* and other villagers, were recorded in the *Khatian* Part II for each village. These included user rights (for grazing, to collect or cut wood and other forest products, etc.) and the settler rights—the right to reclaim land for cultivation with the permission of the headman. The nature and distribution of these rights varied depending upon the status of the groups concerned (landlord, *raiyat* or Mundari *khuntkattidar*) and the nature of the settlement (Mundari *khuntkatti*, broken *khuntkatti* or *raiyat*). In Mundari *khuntikatti* villages, the Mundari *khuntkattidars* are the proprietors of the jungle included within the periphery of their villages[4] and they had the right to bring *gair mazrua* land under cultivation. In all types of village, user rights in *gair mazrua* land (to graze cattle, collect fruit and wood etc.) were recorded collectively for all residents in the *Khatian* Part II. Even in 'vested' villages, tenants had the right to reclaim portions of the jungle or 'waste'[5].

Gair Mazrua Am lands were recorded in a special *khata* and included, which belonged to the inhabitants of a village as a whole or to a certain section of those inhabitants collectively, such as dancing grounds, burial grounds, sacred groves and temples. In all types of village, *gair mazrua* lands were considered to be community lands, which the *zamindars* did not have the right to use or settle[6].

2.1.3 Tenancy Survey after Independence

Legal changes significantly altered the land tenure system after independence. The most important of these was the *zamindari* abolition, effected by the Bihar Land Reforms Act 1950, which provides for the 'vesting' in the sate of all lands, estates and interests (other than *raiyati* lands), abolishing intermediate tenures, and the transfer of all lands recorded in the names of *zamindars*, and other tenure holders to the state[7]. However, *bhunihari* and Mundari *khuntkatti* tenancies were exempted from the ambit of this act by a 1954 amendment. After the *zamindari* abolition, there remained

4. Reid, J. 2001(1912): *Final Report on Survey and Settlement Operations in the District of Ranchi, 1902-1910* in Roy (2001), pp. 358-59.
5. Taylor 2001 (1938): 1218.
6. Singh, S.K (ed.), 2002. *A Compendium of Revenue Circulars.* Patna: Malhotra Brothers, p. 155.
7. Malhotra, V. and Ranjan, R. 2002. *Commentaries on Bihar Land Reforms Act 1950.* Patna: Malhotra Brothes, p. 7.

basically two categories of land in this region—Mundari *khuntkatti* and 'vested'.

These legal changes were supposed to be reflected in the fresh land surveys that were undertaken from 1958. However, till date revisional surveys have been completed only in six of the 24 districts, in part due to resistance by local people. As a result, land records have not been updated in many areas, and the record of rights created during the colonial period remains in force. And where new surveys have been completed, community rights have been significantly diluted[8].

2.1.4 Tribal Land Tenure System under CNTA Today

The revisional survey of the old Ranchi district that was initiated in 1976 soon ran into resistance, especially in the Mundari *khuntkatti* areas, where local leaders have always claimed autonomy from the state. The resistance movements made several demands including: (1) in Mundari *khuntkatti* villages the names of the *Munda* or *Pahan* should appear first in the *kewats* rather than that of the government; (2) Mundari *khuntkattidari* and *bhuinhari* forests should be entered in the names of the respective Mundari *khuntkattidars* and *bhuinhars*, and the customary rights of the *raiyats* in other kinds of forests should be recorded; (3) those who had constructed houses on *gair mazrua* or *am khas* lands should be given *khatas* for them, and *gair mazrua* land converted into *korkar* with the permission of the village headman should be entered in the record of rights; (4) *gair mazrua* lands should not be recorded as *anabad Bihar sarkar* and (5) and illegally occupied *adivasi* lands should be restored during the survey process rather than through the ordinary restoration process[9]. Most of the

8. 2005. *Community Rights in Land in Jharkhand*, Economic and Political Weekly, XL. No. 41, Oct. 8-14. p. 4436.
9. Roy, Burman, B.K. (ed). *Historical Ecology of Land Survey and Settlement in Tribal Areas and Challenges of Development (with Particular Reference to the Central Tribal Belt of India)***.** New Delhi: Council for Social Development, pp. 191-92.

demand centered around the retention of community control over land and other resources, as well as Mundari *khuntkatti* rights. In 1981 and again in 1984, the government attempted to defuse the agitation by conceding most of these demands, but because it did not agree to record the name of Manki/ Munda as *Khewat* No. 1 in place of '*Bihar Sarkar*', the resistance continued.

While the survey was completed in Gumla and Lohardaga districts (formerly part of Ranchi district) in the 1990s, in the truncated Ranchi district (which includes the core Mundari *khuntkattikar* blocks) the survey has not been completed till date. In this area, people are especially suspicious of the government's plan to record community lands as government land, because they fear that even their existing user rights would be extinguished. This fear was, in fact, borne out by the Gumla and Lohardaga surveys, in which collective rights that were recorded in the earlier *khatians* were apparently omitted[10].

2.2 Tribal Land Tenure Under Wilkinson's Rule

The land tenure system in Singhbhum was and is quite different from that in Ranchi, where the *zamindari* system held sway. After the failure of the British to subjugate the Hos in 1834, the Adivasis were kept under the British rule and agreed that their traditional system of governance should be continued.

The system of government through the traditional Ho tribal heads of the *pirs* and villages was maintained. The former were known as the *Mankis* and had under them from three to a dozen villages. They were recognized as the police heads of their circles and the collectors of the government dues, with powers to deal with petty civil and criminal cases. The *Munda* (village head) exercised authority in his village as a police officer subordinate to the *Manki* and assisted him

10. Upadhya 2005, op cit., p. 4436.

to collect the revenue. An assessment of rent of 8 *annas* on the plough was exacted and yielded a modest total of Rs. 5,000 a year. A later assessment in 1854 doubled this rate for another twelve years increasing the revenue to about Rs. 17,700. The Hos paid this with the utmost punctuality. The areas cultivated expanded rapidly and the Kolhan seemed quiet and prosperous[11].

The major survey and settlement in this region was carried out between 1913 and 1918, and the special position of the *Munda/Manki* was reflected in the *Khewat* in placing their names after the first—'secretary of state in council'[12]. Three types of *gair mazrua* lands were recorded: (1) *gair mazrua malik*, which included waste and jungle lands, rivers, government *bandhs* and major roads; (2) *gair mazrua am* (village roads and paths, public tanks, sacred groves, etc.) and *gair mazrua makan*, for houses of non-agriculturalists. All residents settled *raiyats* and Ho *raiyats* had the right to graze animals in the jungle, on wastelands, and on cultivated land after the crop was cut, free of charge, as well as the right to reclaim village jungle and wasteland within the village with the permission of the Munda.

2.2.1 Land Tenure in Singhbhum after Independence

The revisional survey was conducted in Singhbhum in 1958 and 1965. Initially there was resistance to the settlement operations, especially by the Mundas and *Mankis* in the Kolhan, due to their apprehension that their community rights and specific privileges enjoyed by them both in terms of statutes as well as in terms of age long customs would not be recorded[13].

11. Ekka 2003, op cit., pp. 162-163.
12. Tuckey, A.D. [2001(1920]. *Report on the Settlement of the Kolhan Government Estate* in Roy, (1001), op. cit., p. 686.
13. Prasad, C.B. 1970. *Final Report on Survey and Settlement Operations in the District of Singhbhum (1958-1965).* Patna: Government of Bihar, p. 34.

Even more significant was the takeover of common village lands by the state. *Gair mazrua* lands, which earlier were recorded under the name of the *Munda/Manki* or *Pradhan*, were recorded as government lands. *Gair mazrua Am* became *'anabad sarva sadharan'* while *gair mazrua malik* became *'anabad Bihar Sarkar'*. This means that the government, rather than the *Mundas/Mankis*, now has the right to settle this land for cultivation or use it for any other purpose. Although the settlement report states that the lands recorded under *anabad sarva sadharan* 'belong to the inhabitants of a village as a whole or to a certain section of those inhabitants collectively,' it is not clear whether these community rights were recorded as before.

2.3 Land Tenure System under SPTA

The Santhal Parganas Tenancy Act 1949 passed soon after independence provides the legal framework governing the land system in the Santhal Parganas. Section 20, the main protective clause in this Act, ensures non-transferability of land. It does not permit any transfer of a *raiyat's* land by sale, gift, mortgage, will, lease or any other contract or agreement either expressed or implied unless the right to do so has been recorded in the record-of-rights[14]. As a result most Santhals have some landholding, even though often small due to division and sub-division over generations. The Paharias, or forest tribes, still largely reside on hilltops in forested villages. They cultivate land that has been cleared in the forests, but which is not yet regularized due to the non-appointment of a forest settlement officer. They also engage in shifting cultivation or *jhum* as do the Santhals in these forested villages. This is seen as an illegal activity by the forest department, often subjugating the people to bribes in return for such cultivation. However, as per Rule 10 (i) of the Santhal Pargana Protected Forest Rules, Paharias do have legal rights

14. Prasad, B.M. 1997. *Santal Parganas Tenancy Manual*, Patna: Malhotra Brothers, p. 30.

to *jhum*, not just unsettled areas but also in settled villages in the areas, which have been set apart for the purpose by the settlement officer.

There are various forms of land tenures in Santal Parganas as given in the SPTA. First of all there is a range of tenancy and sharecropping arrangements. The most common form is land mortgage, locally termed as *'bhorna'*, in which grain or money is borrowed when needed and a proportionate amount of land is given for the crop season. The second type of tenancy is called *'bhag'* or sharecropping, which is a more equitable arrangement than *'bhorna'*. The output is divided equally between the owner of the land and the producer of the crops. It provides an insurance against risk for the owner and an incentive to the tenant. A large number of women-headed households, unable to cultivate their land, due to the lack of male labour for ploughing, give out their lands on *'bhag'* arrangements, often to their male kin. The third arrangement is *'krishani'*, where the owner of the land gets two parts, while the cultivator gets a third of the output. The fourth arrangement is called *'bhugatbhandha'*, a lease of land that is legally recorded and the maximum duration of which can extend to six years as per section 21 of the SPTA[15].

Section 23 allows for the exchange of *raiyati* land between two *jamabandi raiyats* for their mutual convenience. This section has also been misused in consonance with section 20(v) to secure land title by non-*jamabandi raiyats*, especially in semi-urban and peripheral urban areas.

Sections 27,28,33,35 and 41 of the SPTA guide the settlement and use of wastelands or vacant holding, grazing lands, *nalas* (canals), roads and other common property resources, now classified as uninhabited land, though earlier known as *gair mazrua aam* and *gair mazrua khas*. The right to manage and distribute such land is vested in the village

15. Rao, N. 2005 *Displacement from Land: Case of Santhal Parganas*, Political and Economic Weekly, XL, No. 41, Oct. 8-14, 2005, p. 4439.

headman, acting on behalf of the village, in the case of *pradhani* villages. In the case of settlement of such wastelands by the *pradhan,* this is later regularized by the Circle Officer and *pattas* for the land are issued. These rights of the village headman and community over common property are however being overlooked at present in the case of lease of land for coal mining in Pakur district or for stone crushing in Dumka district in Section 2.31[16].

2.4 Inheritance Pattern

The system of inheritance is patrilineal and almost the same for all the tribes in Jharkhand. Hoffmann records quite in detail the inheritance system among the Mundas[17]. According to the Munda and Uraon customary law of inheritance, the village *panchayat* is convoked to divide the property among the sons if they do not agree to live together after their father has died. A widow with grown up sons and daughters is given a plot of land, generally equaling a younger son's share, for her maintenance. Some money and grain is also given to her to see through till the next harvest. She enjoys a lifetime use of the produce of her land, which is generally cultivated by one of her sons at whose house she chooses to live. Should this son meet her funeral costs, he is entitled to this land after her death. Otherwise it is distributed equally among her sons equally. But if a widow remarries, she forfeits everything at her deceased husband's place and can take away only her clothes and jewels. A widow without sons is allowed a life interest in the property of her dead husband. She may dispose of the moveable goods, but cannot permanently alienate his land by sale or gift.

After the provision for the widow is made, the *panchayat*

16. Rao, N. 2003. *Study on Land Rights in The Santal Parganas,* The GOI-UNDP CBPPI/PRADAN Study. UK: University of East Anglia (Final Draft Mimeograph), p. 11.
17. Hoffmann, J.B. 1915. *The Principles of Succession and Inheritance among the Mundas,* JBORS, pp. 5-19.

divides the rest of the property of the deceased Munda or Uroan equally among the sons allotting a little land, cattle and grain in excess to the eldest son. The unequal allotment of the land is meant to correspond roughly to the unequal number of years spent in toiling on the paternal field. A Munda or Uraon son expelled for sexual misconduct with women of other social group is debarred from inheritance till after his reinstatement into the community. Should the family property be partitioned before the birth of a son by a second wife her son has to be maintained out of the maintenance land of his father. Illegitimate sons have no legal right of inheritance among the Mundas and Uraons.

Daughters among the Mundas and Uraons do not inherit land. After her father's death, her brothers or her paternal uncle have the duty of supporting a Munda or Uroan girl till her marriage from the produce of her maintenance land. On her marriage, this is divided among her brothers. If she is the only surviving child of the family, she is entitled to her father's property and will retain possession of his land till she marries. But neither her husband nor her sons are allowed to inherit her father's landed property.

The *Bhayads* or the closest male agnates of a deceased Munda or Uroan inherit his property if both his wife and children have died before him. In case the deceased's father survives him, the land reverts to him otherwise the dead man's brothers (or the sons) share the land equally among themselves.

A sonless Munda or Uraon who has a daughter occasionally engages a servant to work for him with the understanding that the servant will be eventually allowed to marry the daughter of his employer without having to pay the bride price. If the servant marries during the lifetime of his father-in-law and has been working long for him, he inherits all the moveable property of his dead father-in-law. The village council may even let him cultivate for himself a portion of his land and distribute the rest among the male agnates of the deceased. The land granted to the adopted son-in-law, reverts to these agnates on his wife's death.

If the sonless Munda or Uraon adopts a Munda or an Uraon respectively as his son with the approval of the village *Panchayat* and all his close agnates, the adoptee, especially if he happens to be also a close agnate (a cousin or a nephew), can inherit the property of his stepfather to the exclusion of other agnates. A non-agnate adopted son has to content himself with what plough-cattle and grain the *Panchayat* may decide to let him have[18]. If an Uraon widower remarries, any son from this second marriage receives less property than those from the first marriage.

Among the Hill Kharias as well as among the Dudh and Dhelki Kharias, all sons get equal shares of their deceased father's property. Daughters receive no share but are maintained by their brothers until their marriage. Among the Hill Kharias, the widow of the dead man is also supported till death by her sons. If the widow and the sons fail to agree, the former is given by the *Panch* a small share out of the property, if any, left by her deceased husband; and such share reverts to the sons on her death. If so required, the village *Panch* may themselves effect the actual partition. A sonless widow is entitled to a life-interest in the immoveable property left by her husband.

In the case of Dudh and the Dhelki Kharias, if partition takes place before the father's death, a share is reserved for the father; and the son or sons who may live with him and work for him and take care of him till his death, and meet his funeral expenses, will get the father's share of land and moveables, in equal share[19].

Among the Santhals, the daughters have special privileges in sharing their father's lands. If an unmarried woman's father dies leaving no widow, sons, brothers or male

18. Roy, S.C. 1912. *Mundas And Their Country*, Calcutta, pp. 426-435.
19. Roy, S.C. 1937. *The Kharias*, Ranchi: Man in India Office, pp. 168-170.

agnates, she either shares his land with her sisters, or if here are no sisters, she inherits it entirely[20]. There is also a practice of gifting to a married woman some land in her natal village as maintenance by her father, brothers or other male agnates.

20. Archer, W.G. 1984. *Tribal Laws and Justice: A Report on the Santal*, New Delhi: Concept Publishing Company, p. 142.

3

Tribal Landholding in the Scheduled Area

Tribal landholding, both household wise and individual wise, were assessed on the basis of census. The trend of tribal landholding during 1971, 1981 and 2001 are given in Table 4 and Figure 1 and 2.

A declining trend of landholding was observed among tribals both individually and household wise. On an average the per capita landholding of tribals in the scheduled areas has declined from 0.71 ha during 1971 to 0.51 ha during 2001. Likewise, on an average the landholding of tribal households has also declined from 4.67 ha during 1971 to 3.05 ha during 2001. Tribal landholding has declined by 50% during 1971 and 2001 in districts like Dumka, Godda, Latehar, Ranchi, Lohardaga and Sahibganj

Two reasons are mainly believed to be responsible for the declining tribal landholding. First, fragmentation of land due to increase in population and second, due displacement of the tribal people due to land acquisition for development projects viz. mining, industry, construction of major dams and other public purposes.

A total of 112 Blocks of Jharkhand fall under Schedule V of the Indian Constitution, which gives the tribals and indigenous populations special protection to preserve their land, cultural heritage and ethnic identity. In Jharkhand tribal lands are protected through three major Acts (as discussed above) viz. the Chotanagpur Tenancy Act 1908 (CNT Act), Wilkinson's Rule, for Ho and Kolhan area, and the Santhal

Pargana Tenancy Act 1949 (SPT Act). Under these acts, no tribal land can be transferred without the permission of the Deputy Commissioner and the State must take measures to safeguard tribal rights over their land. However, ironically the State has the right to acquire land for public purposes under the provision of 'Eminent Domain'. Since most natural resources and mineral reserves are found in the tribal area, the State often acquires the tribal land under the guise of public purpose displacing thousands of tribal in Jharkhand alone.

The table reveals that the per capita tribal landholding declined in districts like Dumka, Godda, Latehar, Ranchi, Lohardaga and Sahibganj. These districts are largely affected by large dam construction, mining and industrialization. The tribals have become the worst victims of this development-induced displacement.

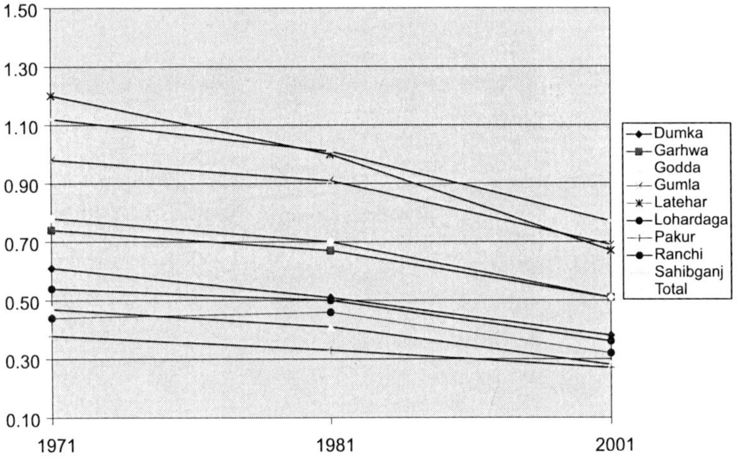

Fig 1 *Per capita landholding of tribal in Jharkhand (1971 -2001)*

Table 4 : Trend of per capita and per Household Landholding of Tribals in the Scheduled V Areas of Jharkhand (1971–2001)

District		*Landholding (hectare)*					
		1971		*1981*		*2001*	
		Individual	*Household*	*Individual*	*Household*	*Individual*	*Household*
Dumka	Average	0.61	3.68	0.51	3.08	0.38	2.29
	SD	0.26	1.59	0.27	1.64	0.17	1.05
	N	14.00	14.00	14.00	14.00	14.00	14.00
Garhwa	Average	0.74	4.46	0.67	4.04	0.51	3.06
	SD	0	0	0	0	0	0
	N	1.00	1.00	1.00	1.00	1.00	1.00
Godda	Average	0.47	2.81	0.41	2.46	0.28	1.67
	SD	0.07	0.39	0.07	0.39	0.09	0.56
	N	2.00	2.00	2.00	2.00	2.00	2.00
Gumla	Average	0.98	5.87	0.91	5.47	0.69	4.12
	SD	0.29	1.75	0.28	1.68	0.26	1.55
	N	21.00	21.00	21.00	21.00	21.00	21.00
Latehar	Mean	1.20	7.19	1.00	6.00	0.67	4.01
	SD	0.57	3.44	0.46	2.73	0.29	1.76
	N	10.00	10.00	10.00	10.00	10.00	10.00
Lohardaga	Mean	0.44	2.66	0.46	2.78	0.32	1.92
	SD	0.44	2.61	0.49	2.96	0.36	2.16
	N	2.00	2.00	2.00	2.00	2.00	2.00
Pakur	Average	0.38	2.30	0.33	1.99	0.27	1.62
	SD	0.10	0.61	0.10	0.59	0.12	0.74
	N	6.00	6.00	6.00	6.00	6.00	6.00
Ranchi	Average	0.54	3.23	0.50	3.03	0.36	2.14
	SD	0.26	1.53	0.23	1.36	0.19	1.14
	N	20.00	20.00	20.00	20.00	20.00	20.00
Sahibganj	Average	1.12	6.71	1.01	6.03	0.77	4.62
	SD	1.99	11.95	1.82	10.93	1.40	8.40
	N	7.00	7.00	7.00	7.00	7.00	7.00
Total	**Average**	**0.78**	**4.67**	**0.70**	**4.18**	**0.51**	**3.05**
	SD	0.67	4.04	0.61	3.65	0.47	2.79
	N	**83.00**	**83.00**	**83.00**	**83.00**	**83.00**	**83.00**

Table 4 shows clearly the individual and household land holding pattern in 1971, 1981 and 2001. For example, in the

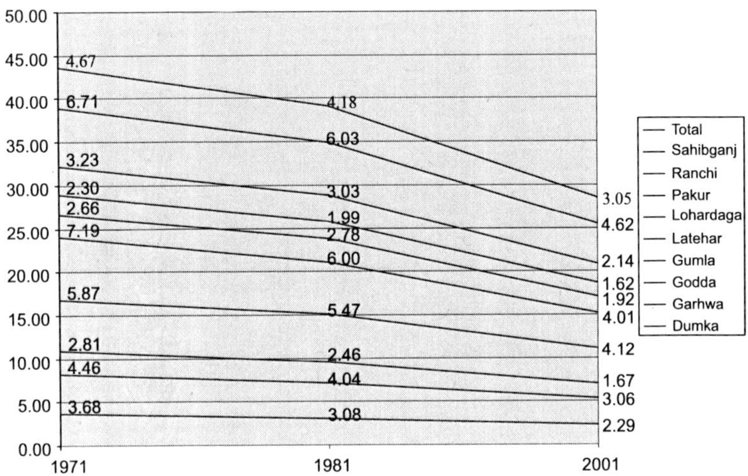

Fig 2 *Trend of tribal landholding per household (1971.-2001)*

14 tribal Blocks in Dumka district, individual land holding decreased in an average from 0.61 ha in 1971 to 0.51 ha in 1981 and 0.38 ha in 2001. Similarly, the household tribal land holding decreased on an average from 3.68 ha in 1971 to 3.08 ha 1981 and to 2.29 ha in 2001. Like wise we see that for the total 83 tribal Blocks, the average individual land holding decreased from 0.78 ha in 1971 to 0.70 ha in 1981 and to 0.51 ha in 2001. Also the household land holding for the same number of tribal Blocks decreased from 4.67 ha in 1971 to 4.18 ha in 1981 and to 3.05 ha in 2001.

4

Historical Narrative of the Process of Changing Adivasi-Land Relationship

The Adivasis of Jharkhand have lived in their homeland since the beginning of the Christian era. Down the centuries, the land ownership pattern has changed. This section describes the disintegration of communal ownership and the class differentiation with internal stratification. It is followed by the nature of exploiting tribal lands through demographic changes. Then comes the political processes and changes in the structures of power further showing the Adivasi-land relationship. This section also describes the impact of the survey settlements.

4.1 The Community Ownership of Adivasi Lands

The community ownership of Adivasi lands could be traced to the very beginning of the Adivasi people's settlement in Chotanagpur—the Mundas in the first millennium BC[21] followed by the Uraons in the beginning of the Christian era[22]. Other tribal groups classified as the Austrics including the Santals, the Kharias, the Hos etc. and the Dravidians like the

21. Thapar, R. and Siddiqi, M.H. 2003. *Chotanagpur: The Pre-Colonial and Colonial Situation*, in Ram Dayal Munda and S. Bosu Mullick (eds.) *The Jharkhand Movement: Indigenous People's Struggles for Autonomy in India*. Copenhagen: IWGIA and BIRSA, pp. 33-44.
22. Ekka, op. cit., p. 6.

Maltos and Paharias came to Jharkhand shortly thereafter. The original settlers were called the *khuntkattidars* among the Mundas and *bhuinhars* among the Uraons. These belonged to the same clan. The lands and forests within the village boundary were owned in common by the village community and could not be disposed off to outsiders without the unanimous consent of all. The traditional system of self-governance saw to the observance of the communal land ownership among the Adivasis. This traditional system of self-governance was called the *patti* system among the Mundas, the *parha* system among the Uroans, the *manjhi parganait* system among the Santhals, the *munda manki* system among the Hos and the *doklo sohor maha samiti* among the Kharias.

4.2 The State Formation Among Adivasis

The communal ownership of land was changed into the state formation under one Adivasi chief called Phani Mukut Rai in the 13th century[23]. Since the lifestyle of this chieftain was influenced by the prevailing Hindu Shiva and Vaishnava cults in Chotanagpur, fundamental changes also occurred in the communal Adivasi rights. The rights on land tenure based on kinship were encroached upon by those who gave professional services to the chieftain. He granted lands and villages on perpetual tenures for military, administrative and personal services as required by the infrastructure of the state. The grantees attempted to appropriate the maximum rights. As such, three types of lands came into existence: (a) the lineage lands or *bhuinhari* lands, (b) the *manjhas* lands, held directly by the grantee and (c) the *rajhus* lands from where the produce was collected and given to the grantee for the *raja*[24]. There was further erosion of lineage lands when the

---

23. Thapar and Siddiqui, op. cit., pp. 38-39.
24. Haldhar, R.D. *Report. 1873*, Government of Bihar, referred to by Thapar and Siddiqui, op. cit., p. 40.

members of the *rajas* family as the Kanwars, Thakurs and Lalls received villages as maintenance grants and they in turn granted land to heir retainers. Thus social stratification was further intensified under the state and made more complex with the inclusion of various levels of intermediaries. The breaking down of the Adivasi mode of production related not merely to the loss of lineage rights over land and the redistribution system according to lineage, but also to the loss of politico-juridical rights invested in the village. These rights now passed into the hands of professionals outside the lineage, and often from outside the region.

And yet the Adivasi identity survived due to the emergence of new *khuntkattis*, at least in the period prior to the 17th century which were not swallowed up in the state system. Rather they were used for bringing more land under cultivation leading to some surplus production. This explains the continuation of state formation. The preservation of Adivasi identity was also due to the lack of percolation of the *Sanskritic* culture to the rank and file and affecting only the court level *jagirdars* and some clan chiefs. There was also absence of large urban complexes in Chotanagpur in the early period and the major trade routes bypassed local markets and small traders. Similarly, commodity production had not taken place as yet and iron production was a state monopoly. All these led to the survival of Adivasi identity in Chotanagpur despite the emergence of state formation prior to the Mogul rule and the introduction of the money economy.

4.3 Political Processes and Changes in the Adivasi Land Ownership During the British

Although Chotanagpur was ceded to the British in 1765, the first entry of the British into this region took place in 1772 when the Maharaja of Chotanagpur requested them to help in the revenue matter. In 1780, the British established what was known as the Ramgarh Hill Tract. Chotanagpur was one of the areas under this administration. In 1773 the Permanent

Settlement was introduced in Bengal and extended to Chotanagpur[25].

The Adivasis rose in rebellion against the forcible land alienation caused by the British. Of these, the important were the Tamar revolt of 1789 and 1794-95, the Chuar revolt of 1795-1800, the Munda revolt in Bundu region of 1797-98, the Bhumij revolt in Manbhum region, the Chero revolt in Palamau and the first Kol rebellion of 1819-20 among the Mundas to mention a few. But the great Kol insurrection of 1831 followed by the Bhumij rebellion of 1812 compelled the East India Company to come to an agreement with the Adivasis. In the meantime, the *Maharaja* and his gang destroyed the Adivasi land system. He acted upon as an absolute owner over the Adivasi lands and fixed royalties over them and used to dispose off them at his sweet will. When the Company ended the indirect rule and took over the administration of the region in 1834, the Adivasi land system had got broken all around.

4.3.1 South-West Frontier Agency

The new direct administration was introduced by bringing the region covering an area of 12,500 square miles (32,500 sq. km) under the South-West Frontier Agency, which was inaugurated on 15th January 1834. It embodied the concept of a non-regulation administrative system under a 'benign paternalistic agent'. Along with this came the judicial and the police systems. The agent, Captain Wilkinson, formulated a salutary rule for the prohibition of sale, transfer and mortgage of land for arrears of rent or debt belonging to the Adivasis. His simple rule guided the courts of the Agency until the passing of the Civil Procedure Code (Act VIII) in 1859. The validity of prohibition was continued in the Act VIII also with a power to the Commissioner of the province to allow such transfer of land. And the respective Commissioners and Judges used this power rather liberally

25. Reid, op. cit., p. 42.

to legitimize such transfer. Fidelis de Sa writes: 'The judges, all non-aboriginals, came to believe that the Mundas and the Uraons were rascals trying to avoid paying their lawful dues. The claims of the people to their land were regarded as false and fictitious, since the tribal people had no record of rights to show what belonged to them and what belonged to the new classes of landlords. This lack of evidence for land rights enabled the *dikus* to continue with their land-grabbing spree. Thus the method and centre of administration introduced in 1834 in fact strengthened the landlords'[26].

During this period of the so-called peace, Captain Thomas Wilkinson, now known as Sir Thomas Wilkinson, recognized the necessity of a thorough subjugation of the Hos of Singhbhum. Accordingly, a force under Colonel Richards entered Singhbhum in 1834. The Hos fought back for three months before they were brutally suppressed. Considering the Ho people's undaunted nature, Wilkinson suggested that they should be kept directly under the British rule and agreed that their self-rule be continued. The British Government accepted his views and accordingly 21 pairs of parganas were then detached from the States of Porahat, Saraikela and Kharsawan and these with 4 *pirs* taken from Mayurbhanj, were brought under direct management under the name of Kolhan Government Estate in 1837 and a Principal Assistant to the Governor General's Agent was placed in charge, his title being changed to Deputy Commissioner after the passing of the Act XX of 1834.

4.3.2 Regulation of XX of 1854

Presumably as a result of the reports of Ricketts, a member of the Board of Revenue and Major Hannyngton, who had been the Agent to the Governor General in 1849 and the first District Commissioner of Chotanagpur from 1850-56, the South West Frontier Agency was abolished by Regulation

26. De Sa, Fidelis. 1975. *Crisis in Chotanagpur*. Bangalore: Redemptorist Publication, p. 55.

XX of 1854. Chotanagpur, passed under the Lieutenant Governor of Bengal as a non-Regulation Province and the Division (under the Division of Bengal), was administered by a Deputy Commissioner. In fact, the Regulation XX was an irony of the said reports. While the reports pointed out that the foreign landlords had made themselves hateful to the people, they tried to rob the aboriginals by every species of force and fraud. The British courts offered no help to the people and suggested that the *zamindari* police must be abolished. Records of Rights should be drawn up and the *thikkadars* must be stopped from illegally ousting the aboriginals. The Regulation XX did not only overlook the recommendations and the observations of the reports, but also acted contrary to them. Special enactments under it were introduced to improve the relations between the landlords and the tenants. Provisions were drawn for the rural police. From then on in Chotanagpur, where the non-Regulation enactments were in force, the District Officer was called the Deputy Commissioner vested with special power and had the superintendence and judicial and executive control over the Tributary States in the Division[27].

Thus the reforms in the administrative, legal and police system were neither well intentioned, nor were gestures of the British good will to the people, or self-contradictory. The purpose of the British policy makers was very clear. They were gradually supplanting the existing exploitative social, economic and cultural systems of the Aryan colonizers by their own having the same objective of colonial exploitation of the resources of the people. This became further apparent in the result of the *bhuinhari* settlement operations followed by the passing of the Chotanagpur Tenures Act (Act II of 1869) by the Bengal Council.

---

27. Roy, S.C, op. cit., pp. 223-224.

4.3.3 The Chotanagpur Tenures Act (Act II of 1869)

The purpose of the Chotanagpur Tenures Act (Act II of 1869) was as usual the same—to quell the revolting Adivasis and to safeguard the interest of the landlords. The first step was to survey the region and make settlement. The *Bhuinhari* Survey and Settlement (also known as *Bhuinari* Settlement) was completed under the charge of the Calcutta based Rakhal Das Haldar. The operation extended to 2,482 villages in 35 Parganas of Ranchi. The land was divided into two categories in terms of the agrarian relations: *Khuntkatti* and *Bhuinhari.* Originally all lands were *Khuntkatti.* They were owned by the village community. After the emergence of state in certain parts of the country, and the gradual extension of its power to the rest of the area during the pre-British era, only a small rent was paid to the Hindu *Rajas.* During the time of the *Bhunhari* Survey, only a small area was available in the *Mankipatti* area in the present day Khunti District, where such land was still intact. The rest of the whole country had fallen prey to the newly formed classes of *zamindars* and *thikkedar*s who, by hook or by crook, acquired legal rights of one or more villages each except for the few lands where the legal ownership still was retained by some descendants of the original settlers. The term *bhuinhari* refers to such lands. This survey covered only the *bhuinhari* lands, which existed in 1869 and not the *khuntkatti* lands. The objectives were the same as other Acts of tenure. They were (1) to prohibit sale, (2) to stop all forms of mortgage except that known as *bhugat bandha,* (3) to follow recognized custom and allow certain forms of transfers to the other Mundas, (4) to invest the Deputy Commissioner with the power to give effect to this prohibition and certain restitution on transfer, (5) to provide for the realization of arrears of rent and (6) to secure finally the record of rights.

The government's attention was concentrated only to the Munda dominated small area of Chotanagpur because the revolt was still strong only in this area while it was thoroughly suppressed in the rest of the region. Furthermore, the division of the then Hazaribagh and Singhbhum was out of preview of the process of the agrarian settlements simply because of the firmly established rule of the landlords over the defeated indigenous peoples there, mostly the Santhals and the Kurmis (who were de-scheduled only in 1931).

4.4 Impact of the Survey Settlements

The *Bhuinhari* Survey began by accepting the legal rights of the landlords, the *thikkedars* and the moneylenders over the land forcibly grabbed from the original settlers. Its purpose was to legitimize the loot of these alien culprits. The *zamindars* not only demanded the land already under their occupation, but also a major portion of the land, which was under the descendants of the original settlers. When the settlement began, the *zamindars* started rumours that the government wanted to know the exact amount of *bhuinhari* fields to exact heavy rent for each plot of land. Hence, some of the Adivasis did not declare their *bhuinhari* lands, while others declared less than what they actually cultivated. On the contrary, the *zamindars* declared more than they cultivated. They procured copies of the declaration of land in the villages and knew how much the Mundas had declared. They occupied the undeclared *bhuinhar*i fields by the usual tricks. The *zamindars* would send their servants to cut the crops of the fields they coveted. The owner tried to defend his property, but the *zamindar*s brought criminal cases against him trying to reap the crop forcibly. Almost in every instance, the *zamindars* won the court case. The Munda was then put into prison for some months. When he came out of the prison, he found that the *zamindar* was cultivating his (Munda's) land. The Munda then filed an expensive civil suit to prove that the fields belonged to him. In order to pay the court fees, the Munda took loans from the moneylenders at an exorbitant rate of interest varying from 15 to 75%. Since he had no legal documentary title for his lands, the lawsuit was always decided against him. By then he was a ruined man. He had no other choice than to leave his home and the fields of his ancestors[28].

Bhugut Bandha was a kind of mortgage according to the Chotanagpur Tenures Act (Amendment) of 1903, which was most dreaded by the farmers. It fixed the time limit to 7 years so that at the end of that period, the principal and the capital were extinguished. But the sufferings of the Mundas did not come to an end. Furthermore, no provision was made in the Act for the protection of the immemorial rights of the Mundas and the Uroans to cut and appropriate wood from the village forest for building and repairing houses, making and mending their agricultural implements as well as for their domestic uses. The Act deceived the people by not defining the term *bhuinhari* land, which gave rise to innumerable disputes and lawsuits. The Act presupposed that the ultimate owner of the village was the Maharaja. And finally, the *bhuinhari* tenures, which according to custom could not be alienated by sale, were not made inalienable in law[29].

The Mundas prayed to the Commissioner, the Lieutenant Governor and the Secretary of State in vain. They insisted on their right to land and told how the foreign landlords had taken away their ancestral properties. But the Government found their petition to be unreasonable and extravagant and the appeals were rejected. Not only the Mundas' cry for justice turned down, the British Officials called their leaders, the *Sardars,* as unscrupulous and dishonest gang of cheats. For the British, the *Bhuinhari* Survey was the last word and the Act was the Manga Carta of the rights of aboriginals.

---

28. Tete 1986: 508-509.
29. de Sa, Fidelis, op. cit., p. 66.

5

The Process of Land Alienation

As discussed above, the history of the Adivasis in Jharkhand has been a history of land alienation from the Adivasi chief to the Mugal emperors and to the British colonial regime. The process of land alienation continued even in independent India including Jharkhand on account of the development projects and the land grabbing by the non-Adivasis. This section describes the process of land alienation in Jharkhand with regard to the following: (1) the forest policies and laws, (2) tribal land alienation before and after independence, (3) political division of Jharkhand from Bihar, (4) land reform, (5) private sales and land grabbing, (6) protective legislation and its impact and (7) the implications of urbanization.

5.1 The Forest Policies and Laws

Though Jharkhand literally means a forest tract, the total forest area according to 2001 census is only 2,314,739 hectares, which is 29.04% of the total geographical area of the state. But the forest cover is only 14% in the state. This is much less than the required national forest-cover of 33% for ecological and environmental balance. The net sown area is 25% and the net irrigated area is only 8% of the net sown area. The majority of the people are dependent on agriculture only marginally. Thus the forests have been the source of livelihood for the people in Jharkhand. But the anti-people forest policies have not only degraded the forests, but also deprived them of the access to forests.

The entry of the East India Company into the 'Bengal Woodland' in the 19th century, and the British colonial rule thereafter, had but one objective of the collection of revenue from land and timber from forests. Consequently, the British suppressed the people's rebellions for land rights. Secondly they forced the Adivasis to practice settled agriculture and to abandon shifting cultivation and thirdly made policies to conserve the forest. In 1856 the colonial government disposed the indigenous peoples of their forest through a government order. It was followed by the Government Forest Act 1865, which turned all the social and common property resources into state property and alienated the people from the ownership and management of forests.

The Indian Forest Act 1878 further consolidated the process of state usurpation, which was started by the Government Order of 1865. The categorization of large areas of forest by the British Government as Reserved, Protected and Private forests empowered it immensely and diminished the rights of the 'ecosystem people' (the adivasis and other forest dependent people) to a large extent. This changed the traditional pattern of resource use and made timber an important commodity, which in turn fundamentally altered the forest ecology[30].

By the end of the 19th century the British colonial rulers had suppressed the Adivasi protests and changed the shifting cultivation into settled agriculture. It was followed by the adoption of paternalistic and isolationist policy as reflected in the tenancy Acts and administrative policies like the CNT Act 1908 and SPTA of 1912. Also the Adivasi dominated districts of the region were put under 'partially excluded areas' with a simple administrative system. This was necessary to keep the region under direct control of the Raj so that the Adviasis could be kept away from the anti-colonial

30. Mullick, 2007. Hul to Raj: 150 Years of Crime Against Ecology in Jharkhand' in *This is Our Homeland: A Collection of Essays on the Betrayal of Adivasi Rights in India*. Bangalore: Equations, p. 70.

movement and the British could have the hold over the discovery of huge deposits of coal, iron, manganese, bauxite and other minerals.

In Jharkhand, the history of 'crime against ecology' can be seen in three phases. The first phase began with the British occupation of the forests as eminent domain and clearing of flora and cleansing of fauna for the production of agricultural surplus. In the second phase, the British conservationist policy was challenged by *zamindars* during the 2nd World War and by the forest department after independence till the central government tried to revive the policy of 'conservation' in the 80s by the enactment of 1980 Forest Conservation Act. And the third place began with a series of laws, resolutions and directives aimed at completing the unfinished job of the colonial masters: to legally severe all relationships between forests and forest dependent peoples, especially the 'Adivasis' or indigenous peoples.

The *zamindars* and the forest officials took full advantage of the unstable political conditions before independence, marked by the Quit India Movement and the Second World War, and unsteady tribal and forest policy frameworks after for about half a century beginning from 1930s to the beginning of the 1980s to convert natural woods into artificial wealth. The British government, towards the end of its rule, decided to take over the protected forests, meant for the use of the villagers, from the custodianship of the *zamindars* by enacting the Bihar Private Forest Act of 1946 (III of 1946). It was 're-enacted as Bihar Private Forest Act 1947 (Act XI of 1948) with certain modifications' after independence. But it turned out to be a boon in disguise for the officials of the forest department. They cleared what was left out by the *zamindars* as a gift of independence and reward to their loyalty to the British Raj. When *zamindari* system was abolished and the operation of the Land Reform Act (Bihar Act XX of 1950) was initiated, all these forests became vested in Government and was constituted as Protected Forests under the Indian Forest Act of 1927.

The forests belonged to the Mundari *Khuntkattidars* having a special status under the CNT Act 1908. But these continued to be considered as Private Protected Forests and their management thereof was taken over by the forest department. The Mundari *Khuntkattidars* lodged a strong protest against this injustice on the ground that the Mundari *Khuntkatti* tenure was different from the *zamindari* tenure. They were neither tenant nor tenure holders nor they owned collectively the forests within the boundary of the village. But their protest yielded no positive results and on the contrary, the forest department virtually took away the Mundari *Khuntkatti* forests from the Mundas with the plea of managing their forests 'scientifically' and the promise of sharing the profit, which was never fulfilled. In 1984 the Roy Burman Commission visited these villages and found to its utter disbelief that miles after miles of forests were destroyed by the forest department.

The destruction of the eco-system for selfish motive that began in the British colonial period was aggravated in the post-colonial era of 'development'. Today 14% of the land in Jharkhand is covered mostly by degraded forests. In the 1970s, a fierce conflict ensued between the Adivasis and the forest department. The main reasons as noted by Ariparampil were: (1) encroachment by the forest department on Adivasi villages and on heir customary rights of forests, (2) exploitation and harassment of Adivasis by forest officials, (3) commercialization of forests and the resultant pauperization of the *adivasis* and (4) looting and destruction of forests by contractors in collusion with the forest officials[31]. The opposition to commercial forestry in Jharkhand was combined from the beginning with a radicalization of the movement for a separate state, where the Adivasi movements for land and forest were always a part of their autonomy

31. Areeparampil, M. 1992. *Forest Andolan in Singhbhum* in S. Narayan (ed.) *Jharkhand* Movement: Origin and Evolution.

and identity movements. They not only criticized the anti-people policies of the government, but also at the same time presented the demand of autonomy as the means of resolution of the crisis.

The government, however, wanted to deal with the situation by passing a more stringent law that would give the forest department absolute control over the forest land. The Draft Forest Bill of 1980 invited a countrywide opposition and finally the state had to change its strategy. Orientalism came back in a new form: the Joint Forest Management. The Forest Conservation Act 1988 is often seen as a departure from the Act 1980. In fact it complements the Act. However, the call for people's participation in forest conservation is not a gesture of goodwill to the people, but a strategy to use people, whom the other Act deprived of their forest rights under compulsion.

JFM policy was adopted by the Bihar Government in 1990 when a huge tract of forest land was already degraded and the forest department became completely alienated from the people. The Government of Bihar admitted in 1970s that out of 29,232 sq. km of declared forest 10,000 sq. km was degraded[32]. Presently, the Jharkhand Government admits that only 18-19 per cent of the total state land is under forest cover[33] as opposed to the conflicting claims of 27% by the Forest Department. Further, the Indian National Forest Policy of 1988 underscored the need to involve local communities in the management of forests; and regeneration of forests and alleviation of rural poverty were the expected outcomes. With a view to assure the involvement of the forest people, 33% of the total net profit was promised to be shared with them.

After the creation of Jharkhand state, the new government reinitiated the project. The Government has a new Joint Forest Management Resolution dated September 27, 2001, that supersedes the Government of Bihar Resolution on the same

32. A Draft Perspective Plan, Bihar 1978-89.
33. Vision 2000, Jharkhand Government.

issue[34]. The Jharkhand Resolution begins by accusing the forest dwellers as the destroyers of the forests. Then it allures them by promising 90% of the net profit out of the sale proceeds of the forest products including timber and demands responsibility to the protection and regeneration of forests in return. The Forest Protection Committees will be formed in the villages, the portfolios of the secretary and the treasurer will be held by the officials of the Forest Department. The members of the committee will be given the policing power and authority to collect fines for small offenders. A detailed analysis of the Resolution shows that it is another ploy to exploit the forest dwellers and deny them any right of ownership and use of the forests.

5.2 Tribal Land Alienation before and after Indian Independence

It is evident from the above description that land alienation started among the Adivasis of eastern India, especially in Chotanagpur from the time of the Mogul rule and continued during the colonial period of the British. This section gives a brief description of land alienation both before and after Indian Independence. The period before independence covers the time from 17th century showing land alienation through the *Jagirdari* system and the survey settlement of the British. After independence, however, land alienation has taken place primarily on account of the development projects.

5.2.1 Adivasi Land Alienation Before Independence

During the pre-British period, the Rajas under the protection of the Maharajas of Chotanagpur not only gave *jagirs* to their courtiers and to other royal service providers, but also imposed forced labour on the aboriginals. After the introduction of the *Zamindari* system by the British, the newly arrived *Zamindars* too forced people to follow this system in

34. GoB Resolution No. 54/90-5244 V.P. dated 0/11/1990.

their respective *maharaja's* lands. Now the British legalized the system.

Table 5 : Extent of Tribal Land Alienation Under the British Rule

S. N.	*Nature of Land Alienation*	*Extent of Land Alienation*	*Ref.*
1.	The *Jagir* of one village given by the *Hinduized* Raja to a Hindu middleman in 1667 was legalized in 1869 and number of villages increased	2,482 villages	A
2.	In 1765 Bihar fell under the British sovereignty together with Bengal and Orissa	The whole of Chota-nagpur	A
3.	In 1772 under Captain Camac's military leadership	Palamau came under a tri-butary chief	A
4.	In the Cadastral Survey of 1902-1910 it was found that out of 3,614 sq. miles only 405 sq. miles were registered as ancestral property.	3209 sq. miles in the hands of non-tribals	B
5.	During the Revisional Survey Settlement Operations of 1927-35, it was found that in contravention to the CNT Act of 1908, tribal lands were mortgaged.	495 mortgages of 465 acres	C
6.	In contravention to the Section 48 of CNT Act, 1908 read with Section 46, illegal transfer of *Bhuinhari* lands by mortgage	The total number of mortgages was 3,307	D
7.	Tribal land transferred illegally due to indebtedness	1163 acres by sale 21320 acres by mortgage 39198 acres by lease	E
8.	Ordinary mortgages of *raiyti* lands for Rs. 24,47,463/- and 922 *kaths* of *dhan* / rice (1 *kath* = about 40 kg or 368.80 quintals)	30,668.75 acres	E
9.	*Bhugut Bandha* mortgages for Rs. 60,000/- and 174 *kaths* of *dhan* / rice or 69.6 quintals.	862 acres	E

Sources: A = Hoffman, JB pp. 512-13; B = Tete Peter, p. 21, C = Taylor, F.A. p. 62. D = Taylor, F.A. p. 70, E = Taylor, F.A. p. 109.

The Commissioner of Chotanagpur issued a proclamation in 1890, which prescribed a scale of service to be rendered for each holding. This amounted to fourteen days within a year. But in reality, being armed with this proclamation, the landlords squeezed as many days of forced labour from the *raiyats* as possible and there was no law to check it. It was found out and the *zamindars* confessed that in 1890 they had been exacting sixty to eighty four days' work per year from their *raiyats*[35].

In 1897 a Bill was introduced and passed in the Bengal Council as the Commutation Act of 1897. The question of the extension of the Bengal Tenancy Act and of the resumption of registration of tenures were referred in this to the Board of Revenue and the Commissioner finally proposed a Bill to amend the several enactments relating to the law of landlords and tenures in Chotanagpur. The Act legalized the commutation of such conditions and services to cash payments on the application of one of the parties. Thus the proclamation of April 1980 first legitimized the *Beth Begari* (forced labour), and then the Act of 1897 legalized the commutation of the same in terms of money as rent additional to already enhanced rent. Now we all know and then certainly all knew how difficult it was for an Adivasi to make cash payments. Hoffmann gives a detailed narrative of the meaning of the money and its monstrous character to the Munda and the Oraon[36].

5.2.2 Tribal Land Alienation in Independent India

The post independence scenario is marked by a conspicuous paradox between the policies and functioning of the state with regard to the tribal interests in the country. Behind the popular face of the state often has hidden its dirty mind. The Constitution of India reflects the liberal ideology, but the

35. Reid, op. cit., p. 42.
36. Hoffmann, op. cit., 1950: 557-558.

bureaucracy and judiciary hold a pragmatic view[37]. This contradiction can only be explained in terms of the changed objectives of the ruling castes/classes of India. Now the want of the already politically powerful Indian is to make money at a fastest possible way. Nirad C. Choudhuri (1965) in his famous book on India, *The Continent of Crice*, observed, 'the Hindu's insatiable greed for money' and predicted that, 'the terrible Hindu passion for money would be the cause of the failure of the indigenous plan of industrial revolution in India'[38]. And today we witness how it comes to be true. The Hindu's pursuit for money has brought them in a big way to Jharkhand. The senseless exploitation of natural wealth, both forest and minerals, and height of corruption in the administrative level on the one hand, and the bankruptcy of the public sector industries on the other, prove the point. Tribal land is demanded not for any farsighted economic and social development, but for making quick money. If that were not the motive, then all these land laws would not have been flouted so blatantly and the tribal people would not have been treated so badly. Adivasi areas, rich with natural wealth have thus figured first in his priority list. This phenomenon is often described as an instance of the functioning of the 'internal colonialism'. What Furer-Haimendorf experienced in Andhra Pradesh can be generalized for the rest of the country. He said, 'It is only fare to admit, however, that in the period 1917-47, the condition of the tribal populations in the East Godavari Agency Tract was relatively favourable, and that the massive invasion of tribal land by outsiders occurred after 1947'[39]. But very often, our scholars and social

37. Das, S.T. 1987. *Life Style of Indian Tribes*, Vol. I. Delhi: Gyan Publishing House, p. 296.
38. Choudhuri, N.C. 1965. *The Continent of Circe*. London: Chatto and Windus, p. 36.
39. Furer-Hamindorf, Christoph von. 1982. *Tribes of India: The Struggle for Survival*, Delhi: Oxford University Press, p. 39.

scientists tend to overlook the development of 'internal colonialism' in regions dominated by tribal and semi-tribal peoples when they take stock of the situation. The cause of the failure of the 'well-intentioned' projects is traced in the country's feudal past and the colonial heritage.

Land alienation can be defined both in a narrow and in a broad sense. In the narrow sense it could mean the alienation of individual holdings and means of livelihood. In the broader sense it includes the loss of common property and rural commons. Land alienation to individuals can be divided into four cross-cutting categories: alienation in urban and rural areas as well as tribal to non-tribal and tribal to tribal.

In urban areas, alienation has been primarily demand induced—for housing (by outsiders) and non-agricultural purposes. This type of alienation has continued and accelerated in the post independence period, and has affected both tribes and non-tribes. The majority of such alienation is illegal and methods include: collusive title suits, collusive restorations suits in SAR courts (where both sides agree that the land was alienated before 1969 or 30 years previously, whereupon it is legalized by the court), '*chapparbandi*' (it includes the conversion of agricultural land into non-agricultural use by declaring it homestead land and unfit for cultivation), '*sada patta*' (it involves getting a sale deed written on ordinary paper instead of the registered on stamp paper), marrying Adivasi women, starting commercial enterprises with adivasis as sleeping partners, manipulating land records and even forcible occupation of Adivasi lands. Transfers take place in Santhal Parganas under the guise of gifts and exchanges known as '*dan patra*', '*badlanama*' or through the conversion of agricultural land into homestead land.

In rural areas, alienation is basically to meet the day-to-day needs of cash starved poor Adivasis. In the absence of active land markets in rural areas, people resort to illegal mortgages and at times outright sales. There have also been cases in which Adviasi land given to the '*bhoodan yagna*' committee has been transferred to non-Adivasi raiyats and where village headmen have settled lands on non-Adviasis or raiyats from other villages for small considerations[40].

There is yet another type of land alienation, which can be called institutional alienation for ostensibly 'public purposes'. The lands taken under this category include major, medium and small development projects of different types like dams, industries, hydropower and mines to mention a few. We discuss in detail below the land alienation on account of development projects in Jharkhand.

5.2.3 Development-Induced Land Alienation in Jharkhand

Land acquisition in Jharkhand as elsewhere in the country has also taken place on account of development projects and the creation of infrastructure like roads, bridges, government and non-government offices, housing colonies and urban development to mention a few. Land therefore is acquired by the government either for its own projects or for those of companies, but in the process the landowners are affected adversely. The main legal instrument for land acquisition in the country has been the Land Acquisition Act, 1894 (amended in 1984). Besides this Act, the Forest Act 1927 and the Coal Bearing Areas (Acquisition and Development) Act 1957 have been instrumental for land acquisition.

The Land Acquisition Act of 1894 is an important legal instrument of economic control, oppression and exploitation promulgated by the British imperialist government[41]. The British were able to theorize and legitimize their control over land using the concept of 'public domain', which was the most fundamental resource for people's survival. The moral justification was that private lands belonging to Indians would be acquired for 'public purpose' alone and that the erstwhile owners would be compensated so as to avoid making them worse off in economic terms. Since the

---

40. Sharan, R. 2005. *Alienation and Restoration of Tribal Land in Jharkhand: Current Issues and Possible Strategies*, Economic and Political Weekly, October 8, pp. 4443-4444.

enactment of this legislation, millions of people have been displaced even in the independent India and Jharkhand today. But because of the spirit of the law was ignored, displacement made them worse off, and their economic and social impoverishment was final and absolute[42].

In a modern democratic society, no right or authority even acquired through ostensibly democratic procedure can be unlimited or absolute. Each right is inseparably linked to a duty. In the case of the Land Acquisition Act 1894 one would have expected another law locating the responsibility of rehabilitation on the state authority to be enacted to counterbalance it. But no such Act or policy existed till the end of the colonial rule because it was never the intension of the British to be truly benign or just. They acquired land for the railways, expansion of the trade routes, conversion of the forest and pasturelands into plantations of tea, coffee, rubber, indigo, establishment of army cantonments and ordinance factories, construction of dams and canals, creation of harbours and the establishment of administrative institutions. In most cases, the displaced persons were either agriculturalists or communities dwelling in the forest or mountains including tribals[43].

The British legacy of land acquisition continued mainly for infrastructure creation in the Jharkhand region,. Industrialization and urbanization were also the causes of land acquisition prior to independence. Industrialization began with the establishment of the first coal mining industry in Raniganj in 1775. The first joint stock company Bengal Coal Company was formed in 1843. A chain of collieries were established after this on the left bank of the Damodar river. The famous Jharia coalfields in Dhanbad district is the richest

41. Vasvani et al. 1990.
42. Fernandes, Walter, and Vijay Paranjpye. 1997. Rehabilitation Policy and Law in India: A Right to Livelihood. New Delhi: Econet and Indian Social Institute, p. 8.
43. Ibid.

treasure-house of India's metallurgical coal. The working of Jhariha, Bokaro and Karanpura coalfields started in 1856. The opening of coalmining in Dhanbad area during the second half of the 19th century and the establishment of the Tata Iron and Steel Company in Jamshedpur in Singhbhum district in 1907 marked the beginning of the large-scale exploitation of minerals and other industrial resources in this area[44].

5.2.3.1 Development-Induced Displacement in Jharkhand

The process of land acquisition for development projects got accelerated in Jharkhand after independence particularly because of the region's abundance of natural and mineral resources. A study on land acquisition for development projects in Jharkhand from 1951-1995[45] gives a conservative estimate of 15,45,947 acres (6,25,889 hectares) of total land acquired for various development projects. This total is divided into 8,52,033.30 acres of private land, 3,48,828.39 acres of common land and 3,45,085.35 acres of forestland. This amounts to 7.96% of the total landmass of the region. Of this, 32.86% has been used for water resource schemes. Industries have used only 11.37% of the total land acquired. One needs to remember that industrial development in Jharkhand started in a big way much before independence. The percentage of the total land lost for industries as listed is only for those units, which have come after the 1950s. When one does an estimation of land used by all the industries irrespective of their age, then the percentage would go much higher. The contribution of mining projects to the total land acquired is 33.32% while that of miscellaneous schemes is 11.57%. It is estimated that the proportion of land used for industries and mining activities is expected to go up substantially in the coming decades.

---

44. Areeparampil, op. cit., p. 16.
45. Ekka, Alexius and Mohammed Asif. 2000. *Development-Induced Displacement and Rehabilitation in Jharkhand*. New Delhi: Indian Social Institute. 2000.

Table 6 : Total Land Acquired for Development Schemes in Jharkhand 1951-1995

Category of Project	*Private Land and % of the total land acquired*		*Common Land and % of the total acquired*		*Forest Land and % of the total land acquired*		*Total Land and % of the project type land acquired*	
	Land Acquired	*%*	*Land Acquired*	*%*	*Land Acquired*	*%*	*Land Acquired*	*%*
Water Resources	364,646.00	71.7	94,808.00	18.7	48,498.00	09.6	507,952.00	34.0
Industries	98,525.59	56.1	63,768.68	36.3	13,435.91	07.6	175,730.18	11.7
Thermal Power	2,598.45	43.1	2,534.38	42.1	894.04	14.8	6,026.87	00.4
Mines	184,169.00	35.7	156,341.19	30.4	174,614.40	33.9	515,124.59	34.4
Defence Estd.	22,543.61	20.1	11,134.93	09.9	78,610.57	70.0	112,289.11	07.5
Misc. Schemes	152,000.65	85.0	8,941.21	05.0	17,882.43	10.0	178,824.29	12.0
Sub Total	824,483.30	55.1	337,528.39	22.6	333,935.35	22.3	1,495,947.04	100.0
Missing Schemes	27,550.00	55.1	11,300.00	22.6	11,150.00	22.3	50,000.00	
Grand Total	852,033.30		348,828.39		345,085.35		1,545,947.04	

Source: Ekka, A. and Asif, M. 2000:110-111

Relatively low contribution of miscellaneous schemes like roads, railways and urban development is mostly because of the fact that much of the required infrastructure in the region was developed before 1950. Many of them were started or completed before 1950 and so do not form a part of the total. To compensate for the missing data because of the constraints in getting information on many of the smaller schemes, particularly minor minerals, local roads etc., an addition has been made of 50,000 acres. However, one is aware that even with this, the total is conservative.

Category-wise, table 6 shows that 34% of all land acquired for development has been used by water resources development schemes and 34.4% by mines. Another 11.7% has gone for industrial development and 12% for miscellaneous projects. Mining schemes have acquired only 30.4% of the common lands, while 18.7% is acquired for water resources projects . The same is true for acquisition of forestland where mining schemes acquired 33.9% of the total forestland, while water resources schemes acquired only 9.6%. Similarly, practically all the schemes have acquired more private lands and less common lands.

5.2.3.2 Tribal Land Alienation in the Era of Globalization

Ever since the New Economic Policy ushered in the 1990s, the economic scenario of the country changed drastically. While it opened up the Indian economy favourably for the domestic business houses and multinational companies, it also became unfavourable especially for the land holding rural populace on account of the massive land alienation for development projects, housing colonies and the creation of infrastructure in the name of industrialization and urbanization of Jharkhand. The state promptly brought out the 'Jharkhand Vision 2010' and 'Jharkhand Industrial Policy', both aggravating the plight of the rural poor. It also promises to provide land on easy terms for the prospective investors for the industrialization and urbanization of the state[46]. That

46. Government of Jharkhand 2001: 4-6.

is why as many as 66 Memorandum of Understanding (MOUs) have been signed by the Jharkhand Government in the last few years giving 3,000 acres of land to Jindal Steel at Ghatshila and 25,500 acres to Tata Steel for Green Field Project at Manoharpur and Chandil in East Singhbhum to mention a few[47]. The State had not benefited adequately from hundreds of development projects in the pre-reform era which caused colossal human dislocation and deprivation of the displaced and the project-affected people, and yet it pursued the capital intensive, high technology driven, large scale and resource depleting development model. For the list of 66 MOUs, see the annexure.

5.3 Political Division of Jharkhand from Bihar

The indigenous and tribal people of Jharkhand claim the newfound state as their homeland, which has had an arduous history in its making. During the Mugal rule, there was no definite territory of Jharkhand though the region acquired this name meaning the 'land of forests'. It covered the eastern part of the vast topography known as the Great Central Forest[48] that lay from the Gangetic plain in the north to the Deccan plateau in the south. The indigenous people of this area had a different sense of a territory. For them their land was a continuous topography, where they roamed about and settled and resettled. The outsiders gave the indigenous people's regional identity to their forest tracts as Dhalbhum, Barabhum, Manbhum, Chotanagpur, Mayurbhanj, Sundargarh, Jashpur, Surguja and so on.

It was due the grant of the Diwani of Bengal by the British East India Company to collect taxes for its emperor from Bihar and Bengal in 1765, which the indigenous people refused that they were put under a separate administrative system called the South West Frontier Agency. Later during the direct

47. Ekka, 2008: 33-38.
48. Habib, I. 1982. *An Atlas of Mughal Empire*. Delhi: Oxford University Press.

rule of the British, this region was put under the 'partially excluded' area with a simple administrative system. Thus its separate identity was maintained from the neighbouring administrative units of Bihar, Bengal, Orissa and the Central and United Provinces of Agra and Oudh.

The colonial rule thus prepared the basis for the popular search for a territorial identity of the region in accordance with the demand of their political autonomy. The leaders of the Adivasi Mahasabha picked up the cultural name of Jharkhand to identify the region politically in 1938. Later, other tribal districts from Bengal, Orissa and Madhya Pradesh were added to the proposed Jharkhand state giving a cultural affinity and contiguity with the mainland Jharkhand. The larger Jharkhand thus comprised 26 districts, of which 16 were in Bihar, 4 each in Madhya Pradesh and Orissa and 2 in West Bengal with a population of more than 30 million[49]. But the State Re-organization Commission (SRC) declined to grant statehood to Jharkhand on the ground that tribal people of the proposed region did not have a common language[50].

For the tribal statehood nevertheless, other factors at play were nationality and regionalism besides ethnicity. Two factors for Jharkhand nationalism were the presence of a broadly common and distinct cultural life among tribes and *Sadans* (non-tribal low castes of the region sharing the same history of exploitation and subjugation as tribals and living in peaceful harmony with them) and their subjection to the same kind of exploitation and a high culture. Regionalism was later taken to be a binding factor of all the inhabitants of Jharkhand.

From the ideological point of view, the Jharkhand autonomy movement was first based on the social resurgence, economic emancipation and political self-determination of the indigenous and tribal people of

49. Sharma, K.L. 1990. *Demand for Jharkhand Genesis,* Times of India, 20 May.
50. Government of India, 1955.

Jharkhand. The first phase of Jharkhand movement (1950-1063) was marked by the transformation of the Adivasi Mahasabha to the Jharkhand Party, merger of the Jharkhand Party with All Indian National Congress in 1963 and then the emergence of about nine Jharkhand parties in the 1970s. This was the phase of ethnic consolidation of the indigenous peoples. The second phase of the movement (1970-80) focused on the radical and left ideology to organize agrarian, industrial and mining movements on account of the resource exploitation, causing massive displacement of the indigenous and other rural populations and the unprecedented exploitation of the miners and unorganized industrial labourers. The situation gave birth to Jharkhand Mukti Morcha. The third phase (1986-1990) was characterized by the consolidation theory of national reconstruction of Jharkhand. Consequently the Jharkhand Co-ordination Committee (JCC) and the All Jharkhand Students' Union (AJSU) adopted the strategy of militant action[51].

In the statehood of Jharkhand the electoral politics had its own role to play. On the basis of the clarion call given by Jaipal Singh the Jharkhand Party won as many as 32 seats in the Bihar Assembly in the general elections of 1951 and 1957. But his next step was the faulty merger of the Jharkhand Party with the Congress in 1963 with the hope of getting the Jharkhand state, which the latter never wanted. In successive years, the different Jharkhand parties kept alive the promise of the Jharkhand state in every general election, but to no avail. The formation of Jharkhand Area Autonomous Council in 1994 was but the result of the constitutional dialogue between the Jharkhandi leaders and the governments of Bihar and the Centre. Finally Jharkhand state was created on 15 November 2000. But it was not the outcome of the

51. Mullick, S.B. 2003. *Introduction*, in R.D. Munda and S. Bosu Mullick (eds.) The Jharkhand Movement: Indigenous People's Struggle for Autonomy in India. Copenhagen: IWGIA, pp. x-xii.

indigenous people's age long struggle for a homeland, but of the political expediency of the ruling National Democratic Alliance government at the centre.

5.4 Land Reform

The major land reforms applied to Chotanagpur include the *Zaminadri* abolition (Bihar Land Reforms Act 1950), tenancy laws and land ceiling. These Acts are applicable to both Scheduled and Non-Scheduled areas although Mundari *khuntkatti* lands are exempt from some of the provisions. Of the major land reform measure undertaken in Bihar since independence, only *zamindari* abolition had major consequences for the Jharkhand area. Tenancy reforms and land ceiling were most relevant to the northern districts with their high incidence of landlordism and tenancy and skewed distribution of land; but as elsewhere in Bihar, these reforms were largely ineffective. The failure of the state to substantially alter the highly in-egalitarian agrarian structure in the non-Scheduled districts partially explains the success of the far left movements in those areas.

5.4.1 Abolition of the *Zamindari* System

The Bihar Land Reforms (BLR) Act 1950 mandated 'the transference to the State of the interest of proprietors and tenure holder in land of the mortgages and leases of such interest including interest in trees, forests, fisheries, *jalkars*, ferries, *haats*, bazaars, mines and minerals...'[52]. The Act provided for the 'vesting' in the State of all lands, estates and interests (other than *raiyati* land), abolishing all intermediate tenures but saving *raiyati* tenures. In essence, this meant that all *zamindari* lands and those other tenure holders were 'vested' in the government. The Act did not affect the position of the *raiyats,* except that the government became the landlord to whom rent had to be paid. However, under the BLR Act, *zamindars* could retain certain lands such

52. Malhotra and Ranjan, op. cit., p. 7.

as those in *khas* (own cultivators) possession. *Bhuinhari* tenancies recorded under the 1869 Act and Mundari *khuntkattidari* tenancies recorded under CNT Act 1908 were exempted from the ambit of this Act by a 1954 amendment. After the *zamindari* abolition, there remained two basic types of land tenure—Mundari *khuntkatti*, in which cultivators pay *chanda* to the Munda and through him to the State, and 'vested', in which *raiyats* (including *bhunihars*) pay their tax directly to the state.

Zamindars and landlords found various means to avoid losing their land. At the time of the *zamindari* abolition, there were large tracts of unsettled *gair majurua malik* land, much of which was leased out to share-coppers by the landlords. Section 6 of the Act allowed *zamindars* to retain land under their *khas* possession, so landlords ejected tenants and kept control over large areas by coalmining *khas* possession, leading to numerous land disputes. Because the exact extent of *gair manjurua* land was not known, ex-*zamindars* also issued fictitious *pattas* or antedated *hukumnamas* (settlement documents) in order to grab land or in order to claim higher compensation[53]. They also resorted to collusive title suits, encroachments, and other means in order to retain control over *gair manjurua* lands that should have gone to the government and would have been available for distribution to the landless. Although revenue officials were authorized to investigate transfers made after 1946, this was time-consuming. For instance, the *Raja* of Ramgarh had transferred a huge chunk of land that was annulled only in 1976-77[54]. Such cases have to be decided individually by the Revenue Courts, which can take a long time.

53. Iyer, R.G. 1993b. *Government and Community Land in Bihar* in B.N. Yugandhar and Gopal K. Iyer (eds.) *Land Reforms in India: Bihar Institutional Constraints.* New Delhi: Sage Publications Iyer, pp. 298-300.
54. Prasad, S. 1993. *Implementation of Land Reforms Legislations in Bihar* in Yugandhar and Iyer, 1993, pp. 39.

A number of problems were created by the vesting operation, particularly with regard to rights to cultivation on *gair majurua* land formerly controlled by *zamindari* estates. At the time of vesting, there were no authentic records of the status of *zamindari* lands (*malguzari*) and no survey was carried out to identify who are the real landholders or tenants in such lands. For instance, many people were settled on *zamindari* lands through *hukumnama*, but their names were never centered in the land records. A *hukumnama* is a written document from a landlord to a tenant granting permission to reclaim wasteland or to cultivate the landlord's *khas* land, i.e. it is a kind of lease[55]. The problem arose with regard to people who were settled in this manner on a *zamindar's* land but whose names were not entered into the *khatians* or other records. When this land was vested with the State government after 1950, the demand was raised for settlement of the land of those who had been dispossessed by *zamindars* and who had only *hukumnamas* or rent receipts as proof of occupancy. Many such cases remained pending for long time because the title was unclear. A similar problem arose in the *khuntkatti* areas where tenants had been settled by the Mundari *khuntkattidars*, and there were a number of cases of people who lost land after vesting because they did not have proper title. This was apparently a major reason for resistance to the revisional survey in Ranchi district. The vesting operation also gave rise to disputes between local communities and the State's rights in common lands.

5.4.2 Tenancy Reforms Laws

Several studies have shown that the implementation of tenancy reform laws in different states have led to only a small percentage of the tenants acquiring rights in land, but has resulted in a sharp fall in the area under tenancy, from

55. Roy, P.R.N. 2002. *Handbook of Chotanagpur Tenancy Laws*. Allahabad: Rajpal and Company, p. 355.

about half the operated area at the time of independence to about 15% today. Thus in the course of the last five decades, the rural poor have been deprived of access to some 30% of the operated area[56] As Saxena points out, 'The banning of tenancy and various lease restrictions has only pushed the phenomenon underground, rendering the tenants' position even more precarious. Even when law provides protection to share-croppers against eviction, it is only corrupt bureaucracy that gains and no gains accrue to the poor share-cropper'[57].

The situation is the same in Jharkhand where tenancy was and is still prevalent. The Bihar Tenancy Act provides that a non-occupancy tenant or under-raiyat working as a tenant continuously for more than 12 years in the same village is entitled to the status of 'occupancy tenant', and that the share of the landowner is limited to 25% of the gross produce. However, because the tenancies are oral and sharecroppers are politically made for their security, sharecroppers do not dare to defy the landlord[58]. Due to the power of the landed class, every half-hearted attempt by the government to record the rights of sharecroppers has been defeated. Moreover, landlords can easily circumvent any attempts to enforce tenancy regulations by changing the tenant every two or three years, and for this reason, tenants face frequent evictions. The only way in which occupancy rights can actually be confirmed is during the survey and settlement operations, but this has been ineffective because hundreds of cases for recording of *sikmi raiyats* are kept pending. Although the Bihar Maintenance of Land Records Act 1973 has a provision for the maintenance of continuous *khatian*, which should include the rights of tenants and sharecroppers, this has not been implemented anywhere.

---

56. Saxena, N.D.
57. Ibid.
58. Iyer, R.G. 1993a. '*Concealed Tenancy: Dilemmas of Sharecroppers in Bihar* in Yugandhar and Iyer, 1993a, p. 258.

The Bihar Tenancy Act also provides that the sharecropper should pay only 25% of the gross produce as rent and that the by-products will remain with the sharecropper, but one study found that in most cases the rate was 50%[59], while people in Hazaribagh reported rates as high as 75%[60].

5.4.3 Land Ceiling

The Bihar Land Reforms (Fixation of Ceiling Area and Acquisition of Surplus Land) Bill was introduced in 1961, but it had little impact due to the high level set for the ceiling and the many exceptions granted to landlords, and very little land acquired. Due to continuing peasant agitations, the Act was amended in 1972 and 1973, reducing the ceiling limits. This Act provides for the acquisition of ceiling surplus lands and their distribution to landless, SC and ST households. Five categories of land are specified. The ceiling does not apply to Mundari *khuntkatti* lands. By most accounts, the ceiling Act was never properly implemented and did not substantially alter the agrarian structure in most of Bihar[61].

5.4.4 Distribution of Ceiling Surplus and *Bhoodan* Land

Data are readily available from the government on distribution of ceiling surplus, *bhoodan* and government land because the Circle Officers and Deputy Commissioners furnished regular reports to the State government; however it is difficult to assess the accuracy of these figures[62].

---

59. Iyer, 1993a, op. cit, p. 252.
60. Upadhya, C. 2003. *Rights to Land In Jharkhand: Laws, Policies and Practices*, Report of Study Commissioned by GOI-UNDP under CBPPI/PRADAN Project on Pro-Poor Policies and Laws in Jharkhand. Bangalore: National Institute of Advanced Sudies (Draft Unpublished), p. 47.
61. Yugandhar, B.N. and Iyer, K.G. (eds.), 1993. *Land Reforms in India: Bihar Institutional Constraints*. New Delhi: Sage Publications.
62. Upadhya, op. cit., p. 58.

In erstwhile Bihar State, according to government figures, 385,013 acres of land were acquired under the Land Ceiling Act up to November 1990 for redistribution. Out of this, 262,476 acres (about 68.17%) is said to have been distributed; 71,542 acres (18.58%) were under dispute; 19,948 acres (5.1%) were not fit for distribution; and 24,288 acres (6.30%) were debarred by appellate courts including 6,759 acres (1.76%) remaining unused. However, government figures have been disputed. The government acquired only 21.67% of the total land estimated surplus land and distributed only 14% of the surplus land[63].

The Bihar Bhoodan Yagna Act provides for the donation of lands and settlement of such lands with landless persons, a responsibility of the Bhoodan Yagna Committee. A large amount of Bhoodan land was acquired, especially in Hazaribagh (328,447 acres), Chatra (210,058 acres) and Giridih (217,062 acres) districts, but of a total of 1,335,739 acres acquired, only 482,881 acres have been settled. A large number of cases have been filed under Section 83 of the CNTA, bringing even these settlements into dispute[64].

There is a clear circular from the Bihar Government stating that when land is distributed, the *pattas* should be given in the name of both husband and wife, and the government officials claim that this is being followed. Although the Approach Paper to the draft Ninth Plan states that preference should be given to women in distribution of ceiling surplus land, it is not clear to what extent women as individuals have received land distributed by the Government of Jharkhand or Bihar. Officials said that sometimes land is given to single women, but there are no separate data to support this claim.

63. Upadhya, op. cit., p. 58.
64. Prasad, C.B, op. cit., p. 26.

5.5 Through Private Sales, Fraudulence Means and Land Grabbing

Despite the protective land laws like the Chotanagpur Tenancy Act 1908, the Santhal Pargana Tenancy Act 1949 and the Scheduled Areas Regulation Act 1969, rampant tribal land alienation has taken place through private sales, fraudulence means and land grabbing by the non-tribals. Often a tribal is compelled to mortgage or sell his land when he is in need of hard cash to meet the emergency needs like paying for the court cases. Loss of land is also due to his improvidence and wasteful expenditures. Moreover, the CNT Act 1908 has been misused, misinterpreted and amended many times to rob the protective character of the Act to frustrate its very purpose. This section briefly discusses first of all the deficiencies and misinterpretation of the CNT Act 1908 and its fraudulent use. Secondly, it describes the inability of the land restoration in the SAR courts and thirdly some case studies of forcible tribal land grabbing by the non-tribals.

5.5.1 Deficiencies and Misuse of CNT Act 1908

Some deficiencies in the CNT Act 1908 have helped its misinterpretation and abuse. As for example the *bhuinhari* tenures were not defined in the CNT Act despite the provisions for the same in sections 10.48, 48A and 49 of the same Act unlike the Mundari *khuntkatti* tenures. Similarly, section 43 does protect lands known as *Sarna* (the sacred grove), *Jaher* (place of worship), *Masna* (burial ground), *Hargari* (land where ancestors' bones are interned), *Sasangdir* (ancestor's memorial stones), *Desauli* (village spirit's residence), *Jatratanr* (village fair), *Mandatnr* (place of fire worship), *Akhra* (the dancing floor) or other lands relating to religious and cultural practices, social activities and festivals of the Adivasis. But these lands are open to encroachment or outright forcible occupation by the non-Adivasis.

The inalienable tribal lands as per the CNT Act 1908 were amended in 1935 to allow a tribal *raiyat* to transfer his rights on a particular piece of land to another tribal *raiyat* residing within the same police station without the permission of the Deputy Commissioner. But after independence, this was further amended by the Bihar Act XXV of 1947 and tribal land transfer to another tribal required the Deputy Commissioner's permission. Such provisions tempted the tribals to sell their lands like the non-tirbals.

Similarly, there has been a large-scale loot of the *Bhuinhari* lands in and around Ranchi City through illegal transfers, settlements and forcible dispossessions. Even the service tenures known as *Bhutkehta* (the dwelling of the spirits), *Dalikatari* (land given by the *zamindar* to those fetching water for his domestic use), *Pahnai* (land to the village priest, *Pahan* among the Mundas), *Baigai* (land to the village priest, *Baiga* among the Oraons), *Mahtoai* (land to the village headman), etc have been grabbed by the non-tribals in flagrant disregard to the customary laws and religious sentiments of Adivasis. One thus finds a contradiction in the CNT Act 1908 that while on one hand it protects the tribal land alienation, but on the other it does not prohibit the non-tribals from buying tribal lands.

The exception made in the tribal land transfer for 'reasonable and sufficient purpose' as per Section 49(2A) of the CNT Act 1908 has been greatly misused too in the *Bhunihari* land transfers for charitable, religious and educational purposes as well as for irrigation, factories and building constructions. It is also an irony that for public purposes the non-tribal lands, though available are not touched. The height of illegal extension of this provision in the name of 'public purpose' to benefit the Housing Societies has been a glaring example. How can the housing colonies be for 'public purpose' or for 'reasonable and sufficient purpose' since most of their residents are outsiders and non-tribals? The protectors of tribals viz. the Deputy Commissioners (mostly non-tribals) themselves are squarely responsible for flouting the provision of the law. In acquiring tribal lands for such 'public purposes', the tribals are not even consulted. Similarly, the compensation and rehabilitation of the displaced people is not taken seriously, uprooting them from their ancestral lands. And when the tribal land acquired is not used for the said 'public purpose', it is not returned to the tribals, rather used for any purpose and even sold out.

The section 71(A) of the CNT Act 1908, which provides power to restore the tribal lands, betrays itself by its last paragraph, which says 'Provided that if the transfree has, within 30 years from the date of transfer, constructed any building or structure on such holding or portion thereof, the Deputy Commissioner shall, if the transferor is not willing to pay the value of the same, order the transferee to remove the same within a period of two years from the date of the order as the Deputy Commissioner may allow, failing which the Deputy Commissioner may get such building or structure removed.' Illegal alienation is always illegal and once the order for restoration is passed, there is no meaning extending time for the removal of the structure. The provision thus not only legitimizes the tribal land alienated before the time limit of 30 years, but also provides opportunities to the grabber to manipulate the implementing authority.

5.5.2 Ineffective SAR courts

The SAR courts have not been effective in restoring the tribal land alienated in Jharkhand ever since their inception in 1969, when the Schedule Area Restoration Act was promulgated. According to the government records up to 2001-02, 60,464 cases for restoration involving 85,777.22 acres of land were filed out of which 34,608 cases were upheld involving 46,797.36 acres of land and the rest were rejected. The possession of land could be given only in 21,445 cases involving 29,829.7 acres of land and rest were rejected[65]. This is due to the widespread corruption even in the courts, which function mainly to legalize the illegally alienated tribal lands through collusive restoration suits. The compensation is

65. Sharan, op. cit., p. 4444.

brokered by the court itself. The provision, which ensures that there is no misuse of the *'chapparbandi'* clause are hardly followed. That is to say no tribal agricultural land can be sold for the construction of houses. In identifying the 'substantial structure' that makes the land non-agricultural, the courts accept oral testimony and rarely order further investigation. Demands for restoration are rejected on very small and flimsy grounds like the discrepancy between the measurement of disputed land in the petition and that which is stated in the records, lack of records, etc. Even if the orders for restoration are passed, it takes a long time before the land is actually restored. The lack of *'ameens'* (officials for land measurement), police force, personnel, etc. are used as excuses. In some cases, in spite of court orders, the land does not get restored if the person who has taken it is influential. Another major problem has been that the records have been deliberately destroyed, especially in urban areas. It is also alleged that SAR courts have been manned by non-tribals who are not well conversant with *Adivasi* customs and customary rights. Prof. Sharan also observes that the pace of the intra tribal land transfers, particularly to richer and dominant tribal groups from the poorer and 'primitive tribal groups" (PTGs) has increased, along with the rise of a new elite and educated class among Adivasis. All these factors have led to the renewed debates over the land question. One view, voiced by people like Babulal Marandi, the former Chief Minister of Jharkhand, is that the Adivasi land should be freely sold to enable them to take advantage of the market prices. They also advocate the idea of selling the tribal lands to the non-tribals for the industrial development of the state. Similarly, they argue that the SPTA should be brought in line with CNTA to allow the land transfers and secondly there should be one Act for the whole of Jharkhand and not two, i.e. CNTA and SPTA. The other view is that the two Acts should be preserved as separate since they reflect specific conditions, that they be more stringent to prevent tribal land alienation and that they should be amended in the light of the PESA to give the gram-sabha control over land, including the right of restoration[66].

5.5.3 Fraudulent and Forcible Land Grabbing

Besides the state as the biggest tribal land grabber, some non-tribal communities and individuals are not far behind in this gold rush. But the data on this are very difficult to obtain from the concerned officials, as they are not willing to show them. One also wonders whether they have them. A study of 47 cases from the 37 villages of 13 Districts[67] throw some light on the nature and extent of fraudulence and forcible land grabbing.

Fraudulent Means of Land Grabbing in District Pakur

Village Chandalmara is a Santhal village in the panchayat with the same name in Maheshpur Block. It lost altogether 63 bighas, 15 katthas and 16 dhurs, which is a little more than 21.26 acres of land to the non-Santhal outsiders out of the 203 acres of land under their control. In the four cases, the Bengali outsiders, who were businessmen and cultivators by profession, occupied small pieces of tribal lands by force The restoration cases were filed, but the verdicts were pending. In Basmati village the land grabbers forced a landowner to sell to them his land on plain paper. No action had been taken at the time of study.

In Jhenagaria village of Pakur District, about 31 bighas of land of a tribal landowner who died without any issue thirty years ago was forcibly occupied by a Muslim agriculturist and businessman. His nearest relatives inherited the land. Some Muslim outsiders wanting to grab the land brought one Santhal woman and presented her as the rightful

66. ibid.
67. Mullick, S.B. 1999. *Tribal Land Alienation in Jharkhand,* A Study Conducted under the Auspices of the Ministry of Rural Areas and Development, Department of Rural Development, Government of India (mimeograph).

owner of the land. But she neither belonged to the deceased's village nor had ever possessed the said land. The villagers lodged a complaint against her and her associates to the police alleging that they were terrorizing the people by bringing in anti-social elements from across the Bengal border. The judgement was awaited.

Court's Orders defied in Land Restoration in Sahibganj District

At Bangalia village under Borio police station, another Bengali occupied some land of a Santhal. The Bengali claimed to be an Ayurvedic doctor, but in reality he ran a country liquor shop. The Santhal landowner filed a case against his exploiter at the Sub-Divisional Office. The SDO ordered the eviction of the illegal occupier, but the order was not implemented. The illegal occupier appealed to the court of the Deputy Commissioner, who upheld the previous order. Now the illegal buyer managed to get a *parcha* in 1984 under Bihar Privilege Persons Act, but his appeal in the Commissioner's court was rejected. So he appealed to the High Court, which also rejected his appeal. The administration ignored judgements of all the courts by not taking any action against the illegal occupier.

The Tribal Landowners Killed by C.O. & the Police in Ranchi District

Charan Pahan and Kisun Pahan of Harchanda village in Block Ormanjhi had lent about 1.50 acres of land to Shri Hanuman Sugar and Industries for five years under the contract called *Jharpesgi*. When the contract was over, the land was transferred to Mahalakshmi Fibers Ltd, owned by Shri Hanuman Sugar and Industries with the promise of some jobs. The Company was successful in getting the Deputy Commissioner's approval for such transfers. But the people of Harchanda village were not given the promised jobs. During the time of *Jharpesgi*, the company had employed only 95 local persons out of the total strength of 1,000. After the end of the contract and the subsequent new agreement, the local people's jobs were reduced to only 10 in 2,000 instead of increase in employment. The villagers whose lands the Company had taken kept asking for jobs, but in vain. The Company even refused to return their lands for cultivation when demanded, but instead lodged false cases against the villagers in collusion with the Circle Officer and the police. Finally, when the villagers decided to plough these lands, which legally belonged to them, the police at the insistence of the Circle Officer fired at those ploughing the fields and killed one Charku Oraon and his two oxen, and wounded four tribals including a lady.

Misuse of CNTA for the Construction of a Temple in Khunti District

The provision of the CNTA for the transfer of tribal lands for religious and charitable purposes is grossly misused. One Sun Temple has been constructed at Tamar in Khunti District (earlier in Ranchi District) on the tribal land through fraudulent means. One Ganga Prasad Budhia, President of *Sanskriti Vihar*, got 11 acres of Mundari *Khuntkatti* land in the Edelhatu village registered on blank paper as donation from one Pradhan Singh Munda in the name of himself and Ashok Agrawal, the Programme Coordinator of the same organization, in 1993. The paper of donation was, however, signed back dated to 1984 when Ashok Agarwal was not even associated with the organization. The paper mentioned the following purposes for making the donation: (1)Development of the Munda society, (2) Development of the Munda culture and protection of the places of worship of *Sing Bonga*, the supreme being of the Mundas, (3) Development of parks and gardens, (4) Introduction of advanced agriculture, (5) Establishment of health centre, school, hostel, *dharamshala*, well and tank for the poor people of the village and (6) Building a temple for sun worship.

The ceremony of *Pran Pratishtha*' (initiation ceremony) was held in 1984 even before the transfer of the land. It was attended by the Shankaracharya. The actual construction of the sun temple began in 1990. Everyone was surprised to see a temple coming up on a piece of Mundari *Khuntkatti* land in the name of Sing Bongā. Because in the Munda tradition, temple is an unknown institution and that too by a non-tribal organization on a land which is inalienable. K.B. Saxena the then revenue officer also noticed it and conducted an inquiry into the matter. Ram Sagar Ram, Circle Officer of Bundu, prepared the report in 1991. But the records were destroyed. The administration was in favour of the temple construction programme. Ms. Anita Tiwary presided over the meeting of the *Sanskriti Vihar* along with the LRDC Khunti in 1992 despite the fact that the organization was involved in illegal activities. Against this illegal transaction of the land, a suomoto case was framed by Sudhir Prasad, the Deputy Commissioner South Chotanagpur, the case no. being 30A SAR 13/93-94, Pradhan Sing Munda vs G.P. Budhia and Ashok Agarwal. Ashok Agarwal was dropped from the *Sanskriti Vihar* in 1993 because he stood against the hidden agenda of the management of the *Sanskrti Vihar*. He confessed before the people that initially he thought that it was being built for the tribal people. But later on he found that it was actually a Hindu temple that was being built and it would remain under the control of the Hindu non-tribals. The Ranchi based businessmen would grab more land on the Ranchi—Jamshedpur highway in the name of the temple to satisfy their selfish ends. In Sepember 1994, the land was restored by a judgement of the Sub-Divisional Officer, Khunti. But the owners of the land remained ignorant about it until one Laldharilal Prajapati came to know about it and informed the concerned people in 1996. By April 1996 all the relevant papers were collected from the Khunti court and Chandi Singh Munda and Durlav Singh Munda, sons of the Pradhan Singh Munda demanded the land back. A petition in this respect was given to Inder Singh Namdhari, the then Revenue Minister, Bihar. Another application requesting for providing possession of the land was filed in the court of the SDO court,

Khunti. The CO did not pass the order even after moving the court 3 times. Finally the DC court was approached (SAR case no. 11 R28/97). The DC asked for a report. The CO said that the construction of the temple was going on. The DC passed a judgement for restoration of the land. But nobody implemented it. A case was filed in the Commissioner's court in March 1997 (SAR case no. 119/97). V.K. Sangma, the then Commissioner, gave the next date of hearing after 8 months. He was transferred by that time. The former DC S.S. Varma became the Commissioner. He asked the plaintiff to go to the DC. Being thus harassed all along, the owners of the land filed a case in November 1997. Pradhan Singh Munda vs State, Chief Secretary, Bihar Government, Special Secretary Land Revenue, DC Ranchi, SDO Khunti, CO Bundu and Sitaram Maru. By this time Sitaram Maru, a businessman of Ranchi became the president of the Sanskriti Vihar after the demise of G.P. Budhia.

The construction of the temple was in the meantime completed and several Hindu deities were installed in it. A priest was appointed who performed *puja* according to Hindu rites and rituals regularly and Hindu followers were attending such *pujas* in great number. Thus, in no way the purpose of the donation of the land by the Mundas is being fulfilled. But the administration is unwilling to provide possession to the original owner of the land despite the repeated order of the courts at various levels. How could the people expect justice from the officers whose top boss, the DC, himself was involved in the 400 acres land scam in Ranchi in the late 1990s?

Forcible Occupation of Tribal Land in East Singhbhum District

Ms Phulo Baske, a tribal woman, purchased a small piece of land (0.6 acres) from Ms Chandu Ho by virtue of registered sale deed No. 6431 dated 20 September 1966. She got her name mutated and began to pay rent to the Government. But one Pagla Gwala, a non-tribal, forcibly occupied 0.2 acres of her land. Phulo Baske filed a restoration case in the court of LRDC, Dhalbhum, at Jamshedpur on 19 September 1989. Her R.P. case number was 7-10/91. Pagla Gwala's tribal wife Raiban Ho claimed that she had also purchased the occupied land from the original *Khatiyani Raiyat*. After the inquiry in the court it was found that the land was truly transferred to Phulo Baske by the competent authority. Consequently, the land was restored to her as per the Order-sheet of Misc. case no. 86/87 under section 46 of the Chotanagpur Tenancy Act 1908. The land was restored to Phulo Baske on 10 July 1992. The judgement read: 'It appears that the non-tribal, i.e. Galla Gwala, has deliberately conspired to fraudulently acquire the land from a member of a Scheduled Tribe under the cover of a tribal spouse. Raiban Ho and her husband Pagla Gwala have got the land in question transferred in her name in contravention of Section 46 of the CNT Act. Obviously, there has been a gross violation of the said provision.' The court ordered the C.O. to ensure that the delivery of possession is effected within 7 days of the receipt of the order. But Phulo Baske had been harassed by the C.O. and other officers. She was asked to visit the C.O. office verbally about 6 times and about 9 times in writing. She attended to the notices, but nothing happened,. She lost all faith in the efficacy of the administration and hope of getting her land back.

Misuse of Section 49, of CNTA in Purchasing Tribal Land in West Singhbhum DT.

The Gupta Manufacturing Company owned by Shyam Sundar Gupta, a businessman, bought 13.42 acres of land from Wilum Kunkal in 1982 with the permission of the Deputy Commissioner under Section 49 of the CNTA for the establishment of a factory to produce screw and paint. The factory however, was never established. It was not even registered until the restoration case was filed. Shyam Sundar Gupta, the Company's owner, and his brother instead built a house as their residence on the plot. The Jharkhandi Organization for Human Rights (JOHAR), Chaibasa filed a restoration case against the fake company in 1993 on the ground that the buyer resorted to fraud and deceived the court of the Deputy Commissioner to buy a tribal land in the name of opening a factory. The Circle Officer, after making an inquiry, reported that a candle making manufacturing factory was found in the said premises. The Deputy Commissioner's court denied accepting the case on the ground that the application was not filed within the limit of 12 years after the date of transaction. It was a rude shock to all to know that the court of the honourable Deputy Commissioner was not aware of the High Court judgement, which had extended the time for restoration from 12 to 30 years.

State Forest Department Occupying Tribal Land By Force in Chatra District

Alphonse Beck received a total of 1 acre of land from the Government of Bihar in 1975 with the copy of the Record of Rights. Since then, he was in possession of the land for 23 years. But suddenly the State Forest Department claimed the said land as belonging to it on 20 March 1998. Thereupon Beck submitted request letters to the DC, SDO, CO, and SP, Chatra to take action in his favour, but no steps were taken for the redress of his grievances. The Forest Department put up fences around the land.

Land Occupation by Fraud and in Collusion with Colliery Officers in Hazaribagh

The Government of Bihar gave Mutra Manjhi 1.50 acres of land along with the Deed No. 84/85-86 and executed by the SDO Hazaribagh in 1996. All the formalities had been completed prior to the settlement. Since the land was very close to the Ghato Tand Colliery of TISCO, it was difficult to cultivate it. The constant blasting in the mines with accompanying dust and rubbles were destroying it. Manjhi therefore requested the management of the colliery to either take the land and to provide him a job and compensation in lieu of it or save the land from destruction. But the management replied that the Company had already purchased the said land from Adbul Gaffur, Shanti Devi, Niama Mian and Ruplal Ganjhu and employment was also provided to them. On request, the management asked Manjhi to submit the order of the DC Hazaribagh to prove his claim. Manjhi filed a case No. 1/88 in the court of the DC Hazarbagh. Unfortunately he died by snake bite before the judgement was passed by the court. Nevertheless, the court of the DC Hazaribagh gave the judgement in his favour and asked the management of TISCO to discard the false claims of the above mentioned four persons. The court also mentioned that according to the law, the land could be purchased only after receiving confirmation of ownership from the District level concerned officer. The TISCO management did not follow the rule and thus violated it. The purchase of the said land from the non-tribals was then declared illegal. The court also ordered to stop any form of use of the land and upheld the rights of Manjhi on it. The family of Manjhi did not receive justice from TISCO.

Land Occupation by Force & Refusal to Restore it Despite Court's Order in Bokaro

In 1984, one Raghunath Manjhi pointed out that 7.30 acres of his land was part of the total 20.02 acres owned by late Fakri Manjhi. Raghunath Manjhi being his descendant inherited the land, but Bala Bhagat a non-tribal dispossessed him of his land by force. The LRDC in his judgement held that the Bala Bhagat dispossessed Raghunath Manjhi with the help of forged papers and documents; hence the land should be restored to the appellant. Bala Bhagat then appealed against the judgement in the higher court, which upheld he lower courts order and dismissed the appeal. Bala Bhagat appealed a third time to the court of the Commissioner North Chotanagpur Division, challenging these judgements. But here too, his appeal was rejected. Despite this, Raghunath Manjhi was not able to get his land back.

Land Alienation by Illegal Means in Lohardaga

During the *Zamindari* abolition, the *Zaminadars* sold the tribal lands illegally to non-tribals throughout the region. There was much harassment in such cases faced by the tribal people. In one such case, a piece of land was inherited by one Sambhu Uroan, nephew and Karmin Urain, the niece of Charwa Uraon who died without any children. It is claimed that they surrendered the land to the *Zamindar* on 27 November 1945 and on 8 December in 1945 respectively. The *Zamindar* settled the land with one Shaikh Karmali Ansari on the same date. But it is illegal to do such settlements on the same date. Secondly, there was no ground for surrendering the land because they received it from their uncle through legal transfer. Complicating the matter, Shaikh Karmali Ansari sold the land to Bibi Hadisa on 29 April 1968 whereupon Karmim Urain filed a restoration case. The court of the special officer for land restoration passed the judgement in her favour. The occupiers of the land challenged it in the court of the SDO, case No. being 47 R 15/80-81. The court rejected their appeal. It was challenged again in the Commissioner's court, the Lohardaga Revenue Revision No. 141 of 1987. The court held that while Charwa Uraon transferred the land to his nearest relatives before his death, the land could not be surrendered to the *Zamindar*. Thus the land should be restored to them. The order was once again challenged in the High Court by Bibi Hadisa. The High Court sent the case back to the Commissioner's court for review.

Misuse of Sec. 49 of CNTA in Land Transfer in Palamau by the Bihar Government

During the *Zamindari* abolition, Buran Baiga and Somber Uraon purchased the said land on auction from the then *Zamindar*. In 1982 the land was acquired by the Government of Bihar to construct a Referral Hospital at the behest of the local MLA. Yamuna Singh of BJP and belonging to the Kherwar tribe and Shibnarayan Pathak of Vanvasi Kalyan Ashram at Garu. They promised the owners of land with jobs in the proposed hospital and with land in the same area on the basis of 'land for land' principle. The hospital was built but all the personnel were brought from outside the tribal area. After sometime even the hospital did not function as the doctors were from Patna. They did not visit the hospital though drew regular salaries without doing any work. Other staffs were equally irregular. Thus the very purpose of taking away the tribal land was defeated. And the promised land for land also turned out to be a non-cultivable plot of wasteland. What was worse was that the Karamachari charged Rs. 3,000 from the recipients for the settlement.

6. The Protective Legislation and Its Impact

There are a few protective laws in Jharkhand against land alienation of tribals. After every major revolt, the British enacted land laws as pacifying measures which unfortunately did not benefit the tribals. Nevertheless, a few tenancy legislations worked in favour of the hapless tribals to some extent like the Chotanagpur Tenancy Act 1908, the Santal Pargana Tenancy Act 1949 and the Scheduled Areas Regulation Act 1969 to mention a few. Because these laws were against tribal land alienation in general, it was expected that they protected the tribal lands also from acquisition or lease for mining operations. Besides, the Fifth Schedule of the Constitution is also expected to protect tribal land alienation in the Scheduled Areas of Jharkhand.

6.1 Chotanagpur Tenancy Act, 1908

The Chotanagpur Tenancy Act 1908 was primarily enacted to prevent land alienation among the Mundas and Uraons of Jharkhand. Section 46 of the CNT Act 1908 states very clearly that under the *raiyati,* land belonging to a tribal can only be transferred to another tribal living under the same police station area. Similarly, a *raiyati* land belonging to a person of the Scheduled Caste or Backward Caste can only be transferred to another person of the Scheduled Caste or Backward Caste respectively within the same district. But

Section 50 gives the Deputy Commissioner the prerogative to acquire the *raiyati* land, irrespective of the provisions in any other section to the contrary, on application by the landlord, for purposes specified under Subsection 1. These can be charitable, religious or educational purpose or for the purpose of manufacture or irrigation, or as building ground for any such purpose or for access to land used or required for any such purpose. Land can also be acquired for purposes of mining or any other purpose to which the government may be subsidiary to, or for access to land used or required for such purpose. The D.C. has the power to acquire land from *raiyats* for these purposes, on behalf of the landlord, who is the State government. (The proprietary rights have been vested in the State under the Bihar Land Reforms Act 1950.) The compensation amount will be determined in accordance with the Land Acquisition Act 1894.

But the CNT Act 1908, instead of protecting the tribal land alienation, ironically sealed the hopes and aspirations of the Mundas in particular and of all other indigenous communities in general, of restoring their rights over the lost land and forests of their habitat of their ancestors. The CNT Act 1908 legitimized for good the land occupied by the landlords, *thikkedars* and moneylenders either by force or trickery from the original inhabitants of Chotanagpur. It recognized the rights of the tribals only for namesake over a negligible fraction of Chotanagpur as it existed then. Many loopholes in the Act remained: moneylenders were as active as ever and the alienation of land could not be totally stopped[68]. During the hundred years of it's existence, it has been amended several times and has been nearly made ineffective in protecting tribal alienation.

68. Singh, K.S. 1966. *The Dust Storm and the Hanging Mist*, Calcutta, p. 185.

6.2 The Santal Pargana Tenancy Act 1949

The Santal Pargana Tenancy Act 1949 was enacted to protect the lands of the Santals from alienation to non-tribals. Section 20, the main protective clause in the Act, prohibits any transfer of a *raiyat's* land by sale, gift, mortgage, will, lease or any other contract or agreement, either expressed or implied unless the right to do so has been recorded in the record of rights[69].

Section 20 however does provide for a few exceptions like gift to daughter or sister, to the widowed mother or wife for her maintenance, transfer in favour of *gharjamai* (son-in-law) etc. and lease for the purpose of an excise shop for a year etc. with the written permission of the Deputy Commissioner. Thus, while the land is not transferable, exceptional cases are allowed, taking account of prevailing customs of the Santhals. Most of these exceptions relate to women's rights.

Section (5) of 20 allows the DC, in the event of discovering fraudulent transfer of land belonging to a Scheduled Tribe, to give reasonable opportunity to the transferees, and then evict them, with or without payment of compensation and restore the land to the transferor. There is however a provision that if the transferee has occupied the land for more than 30 years (as per the amendment brought about by the Bihar Scheduled Areas Regulation Act 1969) and constructed substantial structures on it, he may be allotted that land on payment of adequate compensation. This specification of time limit has in fact created a loophole in the legislation, as people who claimed occupancy of land for 12 years before 1949 argued that the land should be transferred in their names.

Similarly, Sections 27, 28, 33, 35 and 41 of the SPTA guide the settlement and use of wastelands or vacant holdings, grazing lands, *nalas* (canals), roads and other common property resources, now classified as uninhabited land,

---

69. Prasad, B.M, op. cit., p. 30.

though earlier known as *gair mazaurua aam* and *gair mazarua khas*. The right to manage and distribute such lands is vested in the village headman, acting on behalf of the village, in the case of *pradhani* villages. In the case of settlement of such wastelands by the *pradhan,* this is later regularized by the Circle Officer and *pattas* for the land are issued. These rights of the village headman and community over common property are however being overlooked at present in the case of lease of land for coal mining in Pakur District or for stone crushing in Dumka district in Section 2.3.1[70].

Many other provisions in the SPTA are similarly being violated leading to unscrupulous tribal land alienation in the Santhal Parganas, like in other districts of Jharkhand.

6.3 The Scheduled Areas Regulation Act 1969

The Scheduled Areas Regulation (SAR) Act 1969 was enacted to give special protection to Scheduled Tribes as specified in the Constitution. This Act strengthened the provisions of the CNT Act 1908 restricting alienation of Adivasi land and also provided for the restoration of alienation land. When SAR Act 1969 was introduced, three provisions were inserted into the CNT Act 1908 under Sections 71A and 71B to enable restoration of illegally alienated Adivasi land. The 1969 amendment to the CNT Act, 1908 made a distinction between Scheduled and non-Scheduled Areas, extending the period of limitation from 12 to 30 years in the case of the former, but retaining the 12-year limit for the latter. It provided that if the DC comes to know that ST land has been transferred in contravention of the CNT Act 1908, it is liable to be restored, subject to certain provisions:

(i) If a house has been constructed on the land within the last 30 years, the house will be given to the tribal if he can buy it, otherwise the landholder is given two years to remove the structure or it will be demolished.

70. Rao, op. cit., p. 11.

(ii) If a substantial structure was constructed on the land prior to 1969 and the value is more than Rs. 10,000/- the DC can validate the transfer of land but the owner has to pay compensation to the Adivasi owner for his rehabilitation.

(iii) If a person has acquired title by 'adverse possession', the land can be restored but the tribal owner has to pay the value of the land or the amount for which it was bought[71].

Like the CNT Act 1908 and the SPTA Act 1949, the SAR Act 1969 has been able to protect the tribal land alienation to some extent.

6.4 Fifth Schedule of Indian Constitution

The Schedule V of the Constitution lays down special provisions for the protection of Scheduled Tribe from alienation of their lands, cultures, social values and livelihoods and restricts any transfer of land from tribals to non-tribals. Out of the 24 districts of Jharkhand, 12 districts that have a predominantly high population of Adivasis come under the V Schedule and two other districts partially. Since most mining activities are taking place in the Schedule V areas of Jharkhand, the *Samata* Judgement of 1997 can be taken to protect the tribal land alienation. The landmark judgement of the Supreme Court in the case of Samata vs. Union of India, categorically states that the Government does not have the power to lease lands to non-tribals in V Schedule areas. Some of the highlights[72] of the judgement are as follows:

(a) Government lands, forestland and tribal lands in Scheduled Areas cannot be leased out to non-tribals or private industries.

---

71. Upadhya, op. cit., p. 45.
72. Vagholikar, N., K. Moghe, and R. Dutta. 2003. Undermining India—impacts of mining on ecologically sensitive areas. Kalpavriksh, Pune.

(b) Government cannot lease out lands in Scheduled Areas for mining operations to non-tribals as it contradicts the Fifth Schedule of the Constitution.

Efforts to Undermine the Judgement

Despite these stringent measures to protect the tribal lands from alienation, the Central Government through its Ministry of Mines (Ref:16/48/97-MVI, dated 10 July 2000) circulated a secret document among all the Secretaries proposing amendments to the Fifth Schedule. The note of the Ministry of Mines proposed that an explanation be added after para 5(2) of the V Schedule of the Constitution for removing prohibitions and restrictions on the transfer of land by tribals to non-tribals for undertaking any non-agricultural operations including prospecting and mining. This single sentence, if incorporated, would at one stroke, completely defeat the intentions and spirit of the V schedule of the Constitution and open the floodgates for unfettered alienation of Adivasis from their land, forest and water.

In fact, the Supreme Court decision in the BALCO case was a step in this direction. The Central Ministry of Disinvestments had decided to sell 51% of the shares of BALCO, a public sector company located in the V Schedule area of Chattisgarh to Sterlite of Vedanta, a private company. The sale was challenged by the Chattisgarh government in the Chattisgarh High Court on the basis of the Samata judgement. The case was transferred to the Supreme Court and a full bench of the Supreme Court gave its judgement on the 10 December 2001. The judges said, in the judgement that they had strong reservations on the correctness of the majority decision in the Samata case and the said decision was not applicable in the present case because the law applicable in Madhya Pradesh was not similar or identical to the A.P. Scheduled Areas Land Transfer Regulation 1959.

7. The Implications of Urbanization

Jharkhand has witnessed a fast urbanization process, which

started towards the end of the 20th century and continued rapidly after Independence, especially in the era of globalization and liberalization in the last decade of the 21st century. And after the creation of the statehood, there has been a quantum jump in the pace of urbanization in Jharkhand. On account of the rapid industrialization and urbanization, the implications are phenomenal in terms of tribal land alienation and the influx of the non-tribal populations.

Because of the growing industrialization in Chotanagpur, there was rapid demographic change in Jharkhand during 1881-1951. Immigration of labourers from Gaya, Munger, West Bengal and Madhya Pradesh for the mining of mica in Koderma and Giridih and coal in Dhanbad and Jharia was seen to the extent of 12% and 28.6% respectively in the early decades of 20th century. Similarly, as many as 50% of the unskilled labourers came from North Bihar, Orissa, West Bengal, Bombay and Uttar Pradesh to work at the iron and steel industries of Jamshedpur. The town also had about 500 Europeans according to the 1921 census[73]. The number of cities also grew from 8 in 1872 to 16 in 1921 and 35 in 1951, the important ones being Ranchi, Jharia, Dhanbad, Purulia, Giridih, Hazaribagh and Jamshedpur. The tribal population in Chotanagpur was only one third of the total population even as early as in 1891. The tribal population in Chotanagpur was about 40% in 1911 but declined to about 31% in 1951. It was 27.76% in 1991 and is currently 26.30% according to the census 2001.

There is going to be a massive land acquisition for the development of infrastructure for Greater Ranchi and sustainable development of capital by 2010. According to Prabhat Khabar of 19 September 2005, there is a plan to acquire land from 396 villages from the neighbouring Blocks

---

73. Bandyopadhayay, M. 1999. *Demographic Consequences of Non-Tribal Incursion in Chotanagpur Region during Colonial Period (1850-1950)*, Social Change, 29(3-4) Sept. Dec., pp. 22-24.

of Ranchi for Greater Ranchi. It also envisages construction of 80 km Ring Road at Ranchi as part of the Greater Ranchi, besides broadening of existing roads. A list for Block wise land acquisition has been prepared for the Greater Ranchi Project. These villages are from the following Blocks: Ranchi Sadar 37, Ratu 91, Kanke 86, Burmu 8, Mandar 8, Bero 14, Angara 13 and Ormanjhi 27. Total number of villages for Greater Ranchi is 396 as shown in table 4.10.

Table 7 : Proposed Land Acquisition for Greater Ranchi Project

S. N.	*Blocks*	*No. of Villages*	*Total area in ha*	*Populations to be affected*			
				ST	*SC*	*Others*	*Total*
1.	Ranchi Sadar	37	6,206.70	29,252	9,996	55,465	94,713
2.	Ratu	92	23,914.26	60,855	4,289	60,018	125,162
3.	Kanke	86	24,720.71	60,456	5,983	96,514	162,953
4.	Namkum	111	41,993.69	71,480	5,238	27,168	103,886
5.	Burmu	8	2,811.11	4,047	503	7,876	12,426
6.	Mandar	8	2,428.13	6,290	49	4,452	10,791
7.	Bero	14	4,116.64	9,830	183	15,769	25,782
8.	Angara	13	5,701.24	7,344	1,291	15,746	24,381
9.	Ormanjhi	27	8,140.65	8,943	584	17,749	27,276
	Total	396	120,033.13	258,497	28,116	300,757	587,370

Source: Prabhat Khabar of 19 September 2005, Census of India 2001

The present Jharkhand Industrial Policy also contemplates the acquisition of 5 kilometers of land on both sides of the National Highways, which is about 1,006 km for industrialization of the State. There will be further displacement of people in an area of about 10,060 square km. Besides there is a plan to acquire 28,961.05 ha land from 76 villages from the Blocks surrounding Ranchi city. They are Ratu 8, Kanke 48, Namkum 5 and Ormanjhi 1.

Table 8 : Proposed Land Acquisition for the Ring Road in Greater Ranchi

S. N.	*Blocks*	*No. of Villages*	*Total area in ha*	*Populations to be affected*			
				ST	*SC*	*Others*	*Total*
1.	Ratu	8	2,724.74	9,019	1,383	14,562	24,964
2.	Kanke	48	13,620.53	28,877	1852	49,684	80,413
3.	Namkum	14	9,582.95	9,878	908	9,413	20,199
4.	Angara	5	2,928.70	4,080	283	8,513	12,876
5.	Ormanjhi	1	104.13	366	56	266	688
	Total	76	28,961.05	52,220	4,482	82,438	139,140

Source: *Prabhat Khabar* of 19 September 2005, Census of India 2001.

The process of tribal land alienation has been going on rampantly as described above and much more fiercely than ever before. And the players in the land alienation include the state including the ministers, bureaucrats and the judiciary, the non-tribal upper castes as well as the upper class tribals, industrialists, the development agents for housing colonies and the land mafia.

This brings us to the people's struggles and movements to protect their lands and resources like in the past. In Jharkhand there have been examples of the Koel Karo movement against the mega hydro power project, which has been effectively stopped due to the people's resistance for over four decades. Similarly, the people's non-violent struggle against the Netarhat Field Firing Project in Gumla and Latehar districts has been quite effective at least to forestall it for more than ten years. With the fresh initiatives of the Government and the army to go ahead with the proposed project, the project-affected people of the area are regrouping themselves to put up a stiff non-violent resistance. Taking the cue from Mahatma Gandhi's *satyagraha,* the project-affected people are firm on demanding for justice and their rights over their lands.

In this regard, the tribal system of self-governance through the Panchayat Extension to Scheduled Areas (PESA) Act 1996 seems to be a necessary option to safeguard the tribal lands and resources besides engaging in development according to their pace, pattern and ethos. However little headway has been made in the states with Scheduled Area in tribal self-rule according to PESA. Therefore the necessary corrective measures have to be adopted to make it effective.

The sustainable or alternative development measures must also be adopted for the tribal people's well being and share in the development benefits. There are quite a few examples and models for sustainable development praxis, which are pro-poor, pro-Adivasi and ecofriendly and which are in accordance with the cosmo-centric Adivasi world view. It recognizes every beings' and creatures' existence with mutual symbiosis unlike the homo-centric world view, which makes man/woman at the centre of the universe, hence primarily the use or exploitation of the resources for his/her benefit. Organic farming, mini hydro power and thermal power projects, herbal and traditional health practices and the weavers' cooperatives are some ingenious development practices, which one must learn, adapt and emulate.

6

Women's Land Rights in Jharkhand

Since the indigenous and tribal peoples constitute an egalitarian society, women's status is much better among them as compared to the women of the caste societies. This is also reflected in the tribal women's land rights. The specific women's land rights can be seen in the CNTA and SPTA. Besides, the tribal customary laws also give land rights to women. An assessment of women's land rights in Jharkhand can be made along these lines.

6.1 Women's Land Rights under CNTA

Section 3 of the CNTA largely embodied a particular model of the Munda land tenure system as understood by J.B. Hoffmann and S.C. Roy. It included a particular model of the social system and its attendant inheritance patterns. Although wide scope is given by the Act for the operations of custom and usage, it makes specific provisions for inheritance and women's rights to land. The definitions of *Khuntkattidar* and Mundari *Khuntkattidar* in Sections 7 and 8 exclude females (i.e. anyone not in the male line), based on the custom of the Mundas and Uraons in which females have no inheritance rights in ancestral properties. The proscription applied only to the two tenure categories of '*raiyat* having *khuntkatti* rights' and 'Mundari *khuntkattidari*', which are restricted to 'descendants in the male line' and the 'heir male in the male line' respectively. However, a court decision held that this definition was not exhaustive and did not exclude the usufruct right of the widow of a Mundari *khuntkattidar* during her lifetime; although this right is not specifically mentioned in the Act. In other cases, the exclusion of widows from property rights under the CNTA has been upheld. In one case, an Uroan widow who tried to sell her late husband's land was challenged by other members of the community, and the transfer was found to be in violation of Section 46(1) as well as of other provisions of the Act under which tribal women cannot inherit or transfer any *raiyati* or *bhuinhari* land.[74] In such decisions, the courts have apparently relied on their understanding of tribal customary law, which allegedly excludes women of all Adivasi communities from inheritance. Yet the CNTA prescriptions on this subject refer only to *khuntkatti* rights, whereas a *raiyat* as per Section includes 'the successor-in-interest of persons who have acquired such a right', i.e. females or others not in the male line are not specifically excluded.

6.2 Customary Law and Women

The issue of Adivasi women's rights to land an inheritance rights is closely linked to the protection of customary law that is provided by the Constitution and various enactments, apart from the provisions of the CNTA discussed above. Provisions for safeguarding Adivasi social traditions under Schedule V of the Constitution include the recognition of customary law even if it is not codified. Under Article 9, clause 4 and 5, the Scheduled Tribes are safeguarded from the operation of Constitutional rights if they conflict with custom. In Schedule V areas and among Adivasi communities, customary law is generally held to operate with regard to inheritance, succession, marriage and other social practices. This principle has been reiterated in PESA. In Chotanagpur, the recognition of customary law began much

74. Basant Kr. Kashyap Vs. Vishwajit Pardiya and others (No. 1073 of 1995, in Executive Magistrate Court, Ranchi.

earlier when the Government of Bihar and Orissa in 1931 excluded tribal Christians residing in Bihar from the purview of the Indian Succession and to accommodate this, the term 'animist' was replaced by 'aborigine' in the Act[75]. Sub-Section 2(2) of he Hindu Succession Act excludes Scheduled Tribes unless otherwise directed by the Central Government. In short, neither the Hindu Succession Act (unless they are 'sufficiently *Hinduised*') nor the Indian Succession Act is applicable to the Scheduled Tribes. Such legal provisions meant for the tribal people in general also apply to the tribal women.

Article 13(3) of the Constitution recognizes that custom or usage has the force of law in so far as it is not inconsistent with the provision of Part Three of the Constitution. Custom is defined as a 'long established practice considered as unwritten law and resting for its authority on the long consent of the people', which applies to all the people of the local area, particular place or within a particular community[76]. In order to be legal and binding, a custom must have the following requirements:

1. Be ancient (existing from before living memory.
2. Have been continual within living memory (although an interruption of the rights for a few years does not destroy custom).
3. Have common consent;
4. Be reasonable and certain; and
5. Be compulsory once established.

Customary law is proved in the courts through evidence of existing practices, statements of local people, or recorded evidence, and previous court decisions are not binding in

---

75. Mazumdar, D.N. 1950. *The Affairs of a Tribe: A Study in Tribal Dynamics*. Lucknow: Universal, p. 51.
76. Gupta, J.P. 2002. *The Customary Laws of the Munda and The Oraon*. Ranchi: Jharkhand Tribal Welare Research Institute, p. 10.

establishing it. Although customary law by definition is ancient, the courts accept that custom is also dynamic. The validity of customary law has been upheld by the courts in a number of cases. Although Article 13 holds that a custom that is inconsistent with a fundamental right is void, the Supreme Court held that personal law and custom appertaining thereto have been excluded from this provision.[77] A more recent Supreme Court decision held that all customary practices continue to operate until struck down by a court due to their being inimical to public peace or until replaced by statuary law. Also the CNTA preserves customary rights with respect to land, and Section 76 'saves' any custom, usage or customary right that is not inconsistent with, or modified by, other provisions of the Act. This is a very broad definition in that it includes 'usage' which in legal language ordinarily does not have the force of law, unlike 'custom'[78].

In Chotnagpur, the main sources of the customary law of the Uraon and the Munda are the books by S.C. Roy cited before above and Archer for Santal, as well as Dalton's earlier ethnography of Bengal (1872). It appears that lawyers and the courts usually rely on these sources as authentic proof of existing custom, rather than making fresh enquiries into existing practices or interviewing elders about long standing customs of the community. Court cases have generally upheld the 'customary' exclusion of female Adivasis in Chotanagpur from inheritance of land.[79] Although a number of cases for women's inheritance rights have been won in the courts in Santal Parganas, this has not happened in the Munda and Uraon areas. Enquiries about cases involving women's land

77. Krishna Vs Mathura (IR 1980 SC 707); see Gupta (2002:220).
78. Gupta, op. cit., pp. 9-10.
79. In Nanda Uraon Vs Butna Uraon, 1930 PLT 194 1930: iR 1930 Pat 278 it was held that title in *bhuinhari* land in case of Oraons does not pass through the female line and is not acquired by a *ghardamad*. Also see Naika vs Bhuman 11 PLT 194: AIR 1930 Pat 278.

rights revealed only a few cases of such disputes, and very few cases reaching the courts. In one case in Simdega District, a man who had four daughters, three married and one unmarried, had given land to the unmarried daughter, but the *panchayat* imposed a social boycott on him and fined him Rs. 100. Activists claimed that if a widow is given land, she might be harassed. No one was able to cite cases of daughters asking for partition of land, but people may employ various 'tricks' to give property to their daughters, such as selling land and then buying it back in the daughter's name.

The problematic issue in court cases often is not to decide what is 'customary' in the community, which is often taken as self-evident based on earlier cases, but whether the parties are STs or not. The applicability of customary law in a particular case (as opposed to Hindu law or the Hindu Succession Act) often hinges on the establishment of tribal identity, which can fairly easily be impugned by lawyers. The concept of *Hinduisation* of Adivasis is recognized by the courts. If it can be shown that an Adivasi is sufficiently *Hinduised*, she/he may come under the provision of the Hindu Succession Act or other laws made specifically for Hindus, rather than tribal customary law. This principle has been upheld in various court cases, and Section 76 of the CNTA also provides that if a tribal is *Hinduised* she/he could come under the Hindu Succession Act. In such cases, the court has to decide whether the tribal plaintiff is 'sufficiently' *Hinduised* to be governed by Hindu law in matters of succession or inheritance. The grounds for the decision may be the practice of cremation rather than burial, the form of marriage, religious practices, and even social practices such a prohibition on women touching the plough etc.

Perhaps because the courts have consistently supported the exclusion of Adivasi widows and daughters from inheritance in this region, an alternative strategy is often used to fight cases by claiming Hindu status. In several court cases the right of a widow to property has been upheld on the basis of the family being *Hinduised*. (It is not clear, however, whether this right can be sustained with regard to *khuntkatti* land, which specifically excluded from female inheritance in the CNTA). In one such decision, the court held that Hinduism does not require any conversion ceremony, but 'depends on how their culture is being changed towards Hinduism'. The court noted that as per the Hindu Succession Act 1956, 'Hindu' includes a person who is not a Hindu by religion. It held that 'by efflux of time a tribal may become *Hinduised* and they shall be governed by Hindu law', in which case the Hindu Succession Act applies[80]. A claim to Hindu status may be tested by the court according to various criteria. In one case in which Bhumij plaintiffs were claiming a share of a father's property for their sisters on the grounds that they were Hindus, the court held that this claim was not demonstrated, and that as Adivasis are governed by customary law, daughters could not inherit the property of the father or mother.[81] As the above decision suggests, the customary law of all Adivasis in Chotanagpur is presumed by the courts to disinherit women, although in this case no authority was cited to support this presumption.

The mater is somewhat more straightforward in the case of conversion to Christianity. In Kartick Oraon Vs. David Munzni (AIR 1964 Pat 201), the court held that the Scheduled Tribe status is not lost due to conversion to Christianity in the matter of inheritance.[82] It has been a settled law throughout India that an Adviasi retains his/her ST status

80. Dhanai Majhi and Others Vs Ranga Majhi and Others, 1999(1) PLJR 605: 1999 (1) BLJR 695.
81. Gopal Singh Bhumij Vs Giribala bhumij and others, AIR 1991 Patna 138. Interestingly, the court argued that the plaintiff would have to prove not only that his/her own family is *Hinduised*, but that other Bhumijs of the same or neighbouring villages have also adopted the Hindu religion and follow its rites and practices.
82. The case concerned *bhuuinhars* who became Christians and it was disputed whether they could become the *pahan* of a village (see Roy 2002:201).

regardless of his/her religion (unlike the SCs, who can remain SC only as a Hindu or Sikh). Also, an ST does not lose ST status by marriage or migration, nor does a non-ST in a recent case that is pending in the High Court concerning a Christian Munda girl married to a Nepali Christian boy. She purchased land from another tribal and a case was filed against her under Section 46 on the grounds that she was not a tribal because she was Christian. Her lawyers argued successfully in the lower court that marriage does not dissolve her identity, but the decision was appealed.

Another facet of the question of tribal identity and custom was raised in a recent case (not concerned with property, but with accessing benefits available to STs) regarding the status of children born out of wedlock from a tribal woman and non-tribal man. The court held that the children could have the status of ST provided that 'the society of the Tribes to which the woman belongs has recognized such matrimonial alliance and accepts the couple into their fold'.[83] This decision was based on precedents, perhaps beginning with a 1972 election dispute case in which the Supreme Court decided that if a tribal man marries a non-ST woman and the marriage is approved by the tribal people and the woman is accepted into the tribe, she would get the benefits of reservation.[84] This is a contentious issue, given that in many Adivasi communities, both men and women can be ostracized for marrying outside the community, and men may as a result lose their right of inheritance. According to S.C. Roy, among the Mundas if a son is made an outcaste due to marriage with a non-Munda, he is not entitled to a share of partition, unless he has been reinstated in the community by the *panchayat* 'after he has given up his alien wife'[85]. Among the

83. Society for Protection and Enforcement of *Adivasi* Rights and Others Vs. The State and Others, 2001 (2) JLJR 222.
84. NE Horo Vs. Smt Jahan Ara Jaipal Singh (AIR 1972, SC 1840), quoted in Gupta (2002:173).
85. Roy, S.C, 1912. op. cit., 246.

Oraons, on the other hand, even a 'disobedient' son disowned by his father cannot be denied his share[86]. In some cases the court held that the offspring of a Munda man and non-Munda woman is illegitimate and cannot inherit.[87]

---

86. Roy, S.C 1937. op. cit., 215.
87. Madhusudan Singh Munda and others Vs. Darnay Bhushan Singh Munda and Others. LPA No. 4 of AIR, Patna 144 (Ranchi Bench), decided on 14.10.98 (Gupta 2002: 98).

7

Nature of Land Use

The lure of the increased productivity through the use of the high yielding variety seeds and chemical fertilizers has brought about much damange to the soils of Jharkhand. This section deals with the nature of land use in the state. Not much data is available on this topic since 2000 when Jharkhand became a separate state. Therefore, the available data when it the state was part of Bihar is relied upon. The brief description on the nature of land use pertain to the soil problems due to fertilizer and pesticide, operational land holdings in 1995-96 and area, production and productivity of the food grains in Jharkhand.

Soil Problems due to Fertilizer and Pesticide use

About 30% of the soil of the plateau region is deficient in potassium, which is even less than the critical limit. There were instances of Boron deficiency in the soils. Long term application of Nitrogenous fertilizers alone has resulted in the removal and consequent depletion of micronutrients. The red soils of Jharkhand under the maize and the wheat cropping systems continuously fertilized with Ammonium Sulphate for 34 years have turned the soil into highly acidic type. 49% of the total soil is highly acidic and about 36% of the soil is moderately acidic.

There were evidences of pesticide residues in the soil, mostly of Endosulphan, which was higher than the recommended level. Most of the vegetables were contaminated with Endosulphan[88].

Operational Land Holdings in 1995-96

In the absence of the data on land holding pattern after the creation of the state, the latest data of 1995-96 when it was a part of Bihar is relied upon. The operational land holding pattern of Bihar during this time is given in table 9.

Table 9 : Land Holding Pattern of Bihar including Jharkhand in 1995-96

(Numbers are in 1000)

Land Holding Category	*Bihar*	*All India*	*Percentage of Bihar of All India*
Marginal	11,344 (80.141)	71,179	15.93
Small	1,526 (10.780)	21,643	7.05
Semi-medium	941 (6.647)	14,261	6.59
Medium	314 (2.218)	7,092	4.42
Large	29 (0.204)	1,404	2.06
Total	14,154 (100)	115,579	12.24

(*Source*: Agricultural Marketing Statistical Abstract, 2004; National Institute of Agricultural Marketing, Jaipur, Government of India)

The marginal holding constituted about 80% of the total holding in Bihar. The small, semi-medium and medium holdings were 10.78%, 6.65% and 2.22% respectively. However, the large holding was only 0.20% of the total operational holdings of Bihar.

Area, Production and Productivity of Food Grains

Jharkhand has the total geographical area of 79.70 Lakh ha out of which the cultivable land, net sown area and net irrigated area are 38.00 Lakh ha, 18.04 Lakh ha and 01.57 Lakh

88. ISSS & BAU, 2007. *72nd Annual Convention of the Indian Society of Soil Science and National Seminar on 'Development in Soil Science: 2007'*, organised by Ranchi Chapter of Indian Society of Soil Science and Birsa Agricultural University, Ranchi.

ha respectively. Forest area is about 29% and the net sown area is 25% of total area.

The average production in Jharkhand was 20,08,500 tonnes, which was only 0.95% of the total food grain production in India in 2003-04. The average productivity of food grains in Jharkhand was 1,094 kg/ha, while the average productivity of food grains in India was 1,740 kg/ha during the same period, i.e. the food grain productivity of Jharkhand was 38% lesser than the national average food grain productivity. However, the food grain production and productivity have increased substantially over the years from 1972-73 to 2001-02. The increase in the productivity of the food grain over the years was nearly 50% during 1972-73 to 2001-02 but much lesser than in average increase in the national productivity of 114% over the same period. The increase in the production of the food grains in Jharkhand from 1972-73 to 2001-02 was 118%. A similar trend was found on national production of food grains (118% increase). The increase in production of food grains over the years was due to the increase in the productivity and increased crop production area. By 2001-02, the area under production in Jharkhand was 1,835,900 ha with an increase of about 25% over the years from 1972-73 to 2001-02, which was much higher than the average Indian increase of 2.2% over the same

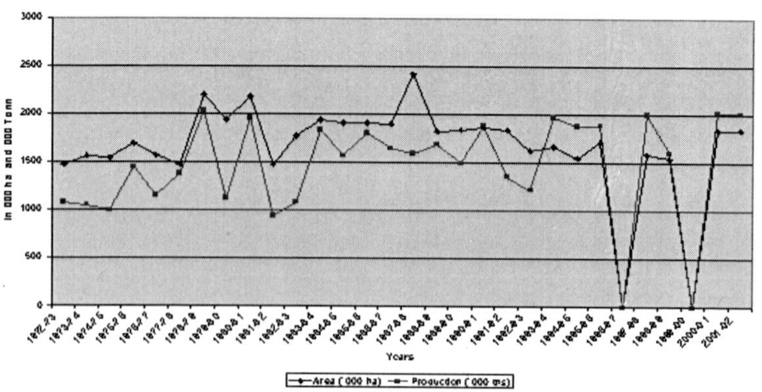

Fig. 3 *Production and Area under food grains in Jharkhand*

Table 10 : Production and Productivity of Food Grains in Jharkhand

Year	*Jharkhand*			*India*		
	Area ('000 ha)	*Production ('000 tns)*	*Yield (Kg/ha)*	*Area ('000 ha)*	*Production (Kg/ha)*	*Yield ('000 tns)*
1972-73	1,472.7	1,074.9	730	119,277	97,026.3	814
1973-74	1,566.6	1,052.9	672	126,538	104,665.0	827
1974-75	1,543.7	995.1	645	121,075	99,826.2	824
1975-76	1,693.1	1,450.2	857	128,181	121,034.0	944
1976-77	1,571.2	1,155.2	735	124,356	111,167.0	894
1977-78	1,474.4	1,383.1	938	127,515	126,407.0	991
1978-79	2,199.6	2,027.9	922	129,009	131,902.0	1,022
1979-80	1,936.2	1,124.5	581	125,206	109,700.0	876
1980-81	2,180.6	1,955.2	897	125,790	129,867.0	1,032
1981-82	1,475.7	943.3	639	129,138	133,295.0	1,032
1982-83	1,773.2	1,085.2	612	125,095	129,519.0	1,035
1983-84	1,936.3	1,832.6	946	131,163	152,374.0	1,162
1984-85	1,906.7	1,572.3	825	126,673	145,539.0	1,149
1985-86	1,908.8	1,801.0	944	128,023	150,440.0	1,175
1986-87	1,896.1	1,646.1	868	127,195	143,418.0	1,128
1987-88	2,418.2	1,593.6	659	119,696	140,354.0	1,173
1988-89	1822	1,687.5	926	127,675	169,922.0	1,331
1989-90	1,839.2	1,498.0	814	126,773	171,036.0	1,349
1990-91	1,868.3	1,883.9	1,008	127,835	176,390.0	1,380
1991-92	1,836.8	1,354.2	737	121,871	168,380.0	1,382
1992-93	1,628.2	1,218.9	749	123,148	179,480.0	1,457
1993-94	1,666.1	1,967.0	1,181	122,754	184,260.0	1,501
1994-95	1,550.1	1,879.8	1,213	123,860	191,494.0	1,546
1995-96	1,711.7	1,883.3	1,100	121,015	180,414.0	1,491
1996-97	0	0	0	123,581	199,436.0	1,614
1997-98	1,587.1	1,996.3	1,260	123,847	192,260.0	1,552
1998-99	1,541.5	1,599.5	1,040	125,167	203,607.0	1,627
1999-00	0	0	0	123,104	209,802.0	1,704
2000-01	1,836.0	2,011.0	1,095	121,050	196,810.0	1,630
2001-02	1,835.9	2,008.5	1,094	121,912	212,034.0	1,740

Source: Agricultural Marketing Statistical Abstract, 2004; National Institute of Agricultural Marketing, Jaipur, Government of India

period. By 1972-73, the area under production was 1.23% of the total food grain crops of India, but by 2001-02, the total area under the food grain was 1.5% of the total national area under food grain crops.

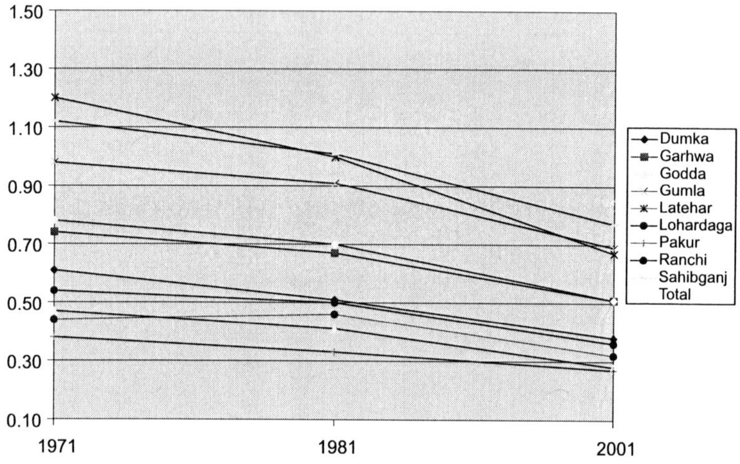

Fig. 4 *Per capita landholding of tribal in Jharkhand (1971 -2001)*

The kharif food grain production was 1,892,300 tonnes in 2001-02. In the same year, the kharif food grain productivity was 1,076 kg/ha, which was lower than the average food grain productivity of the state (1,094 kg/ha). The kharif production was about 1,892,300 tonnes, about 116,200 tonnes lesser than the total food grains productions of the state. The area under production of food grain crops in 2001-02 was 1,759,400 ha, about 76,500 ha lesser than the total area under food grain crops.

8

Conclusion

This comprehensive study on Adivasi lands in Jharkhand dealt with the tribal demography, land tenures, land holding pattern, the historical narratives of the processes of changing Adivasi-land relationship, details of land alienation, land reform, impact of urbanization on Adivasi lands, women's land rights and the nature of land use.

It gives an idea of the Adivasi lands in Jharkhand in a historical perspective. The Adivasi lands and forest resources have been expropriated by the non-Adivasi rulers and peoples from time immemorial, causing irreparable damage to their socio-economic and politico-cultural systems. The process of Adivasi land alienation continues much more rampantly today than ever before. This has caused a severe threat to the Adivasi people's very existence and identity. The gradual increase of the non-Adivasi population in Jharkhand and the anti-tribal policies of the government have further aggravated the situation. The irony is that while on one hand there is an increase in the migration of the Adivasis to cities in search of livelihoods, mostly through unskilled jobs, there is an a heavy influx of the non-Adivasi populations to Jharkhand due to the growing prospects of industrialization and urbanization on the other.

Similarly, the expectations of the tribal people's governance and development of their new found state since 2000 have been belied due to the corrupt practices and political hegemony of the anti-tribal political parties. Due to the lack of vision and sense of purpose of the dominating political parties, no tribal Chief Minister has been able to change the deteriorating condition of Jharkhand. Consequently, after the failure of the governance of the seven Chief Ministers in the eight years of the state's inception, the President's rule has been imposed on Jharkhand. In such a state of affairs, the Adivasi land situation in Jharkhand is going to be more precarious.

In such a situation one thinks of the Adivasi struggles and movements to protect the Adivasi lands and resources as done in the past. Adivasis are in fact resorting to this strategy to safeguard their lands and forests. The two instances of the Koel Karo and the Neterhat movements can be reiterated. After a long struggle of about 40 years against the mega hydro power project, the local people have nearly forced the government to shelve it. Similarly, through the fifteen-year long *Satyagraha* and non-violent movement against the field firing project at Netharhat, the project-affected people so far have been able to resist the impending project. Their resolve is to force the government to abandon it. There are many such cases of people's movements against displacement and land alienation in the state, but not all are able to sustain the police brutality and government high-handedness.

While such struggles and movements against displacement must continue, other measures must also be adopted to protect Adivasi lands and resources. In this regard, the local self-governance through the provisions of the Panchayat Extension to the Scheduled Areas (PESA) Act 1996 is recommended. In many aspects, the tribal self rule through PESA has been quite effective in Maharashtra, Rajasthan and Himachal Pradesh despite the fact that many of the state laws in this regard are not in full conformity with the PESA Act as desired. In Jharkhand the situation is not impressive due to the weak Panchayati Raj Legislation and its poor implementation. Therefore a thorough amendment of this Act is required in the state and the mobilization of the people to implement it.

Besides adopting these measures, it is also suggested that the Adivasis must be encouraged to opt for sustainable or alternative development practices like organic farming for agriculture, the community based mini hydro and thermal power projects for power generation, herbal and traditional medical practices for health care and the weavers' cooperatives in the cottage industries sector.

It is expected that this study further helps in awareness building on the Adivasi land question in Jharkhand and for appropriate action on behalf of the people. It is also expected that it helps in policy changes of the government regarding the protection of Adivasi lands and forests and in adopting appropriate development interventions among the tribals.

References

Agricultural Marketing Statistical Abstract, 2004. National Institute of Agricultural Marketing, Jaipur, Government of India.

Areeparampil, M. 1992. *Forest Andolan in Singhbhum* in S. Narayan (ed.) *Jharkhand Movement: Origin and Evolution.*

Archer, W.G. 1984. *Tribal Laws and Justice: A Report on the Santal,* New Delhi: Concept Publishing Company.

Bandyopadhayay, M. 1999. *Demographic Consequences of Non-Tribal Incursion in Chotanagpur Region during Colonial Period (1850-1950),* Social Change, 29(3-4) Sept. Dec. 1999.

Choudhuri, N.C. 1965. *The Continent of Circe.* London: Chatto and Windus.

Das, S.T. 1987. *Life Style of Indian Tribes,* Vol. I. Delhi: Gyan Publishing House.

De Sa, Fidelis. 1975. *Crisis in Chotanagpur,* Bangalore: Redemptorist Publication.

Ekka, Alexius and Mohammed Asif. 2000. *Development-Induced Displacement and Rehabilitation in Jharkhand.* New Delhi: Indian Social Institute. 2000.

Ekka, P. 2003. *Tribal Movements: A Study in Social Change.* Pathalgaon: Tribal Research and Documentation Centre.

Fernandes, Walter, and Vijay Paranjpye. 1997. Rehabilitation Policy and Law in India: A Right to Livelihood. New Delhi: Econet and Indian Social Institute, p. 8.

Furer-Hamindorf, Christoph von. 1982. *Tribes of India: The Struggle for Survival.* Delhi: Oxford University Press.

GOI, 1955. *Report of the States Reorganization Commission,* New Delhi.

Gupta, J.P. 2002. *The Customary Laws of the Munda and the Oraon.* Ranchi: Jharkhand Tribal Welare Research Institute.

Habib, I. 1982. *An Atlas of Mughal Empire*. Delhi: Oxford University Press.

Haldhar, R.D. *Report. 1873*, Government of Bihar, referred to by Thapar and Siddiqui, op. cit.

Hoffmann, J.B. 1915. *The Principles of Succession and Inheritance among the Mundas*, JBORS.

ISSS & BAU, 2007. *72nd Annual Convention of the Indian Society of Soil Science and National Seminar on 'Development in Soil Science: 2007'*, organised by Ranchi Chapter of Indian Society of Soil Science and Birsa Agricultural University, Ranchi.

Iyer, R.G. 1993a. *'Concealed Tenancy: Dilemmas of Sharecroppers in Bihar* in Yugandhar and Iyer, 1993a, *op. cit*. pp. 247-265.

——— 1993b. *Government and Community Land in Bihar* in B.N. Yugandhar and Copal K. Iyer (eds.*) Land Reforms in India: Bihar Institutional Constraints*. New Delhi: Sage Publications.

Louis, Prakash. 2007. *Tribals of Jharkhand at Crossroads* in Joseph Marianus Kujur and Sonajharia Minz (eds.) *Indigenous People of India: Problems and Prospects (Essays in Honour of Bishop Dr. Nirmal Minz, an Adivasi Intellectual)*. New Delhi: Indian Social Institute, pp. 138-155.

Malhotra. V. and Ranjan R. 2002. *Commentaries on Bihar Land Reforms Act 1950*. Patna: Malhotra Brothers.

Mazumdar, D.N. 1950. *The Affairs of a Tribe: A Study in Tribal Dynamics*. Lucknow: Universal.

Mullick, S.B. 1999. *Tribal Land Alienation in Jharkhand*, A Study Conducted under the Auspices of the Ministry of Rural Areas and Development, Department of Rural Development, Government of India (mimeograph).

——— 2003. *Introduction*, in R.D. Munda and S. Bosu Mullick (eds.) The Jharkhand Movement: Indigenous People's Struggle for Autonomy in India. Copenhagen: IWGIA.

——— 2007. Hul to Raj: 150 Years of Crime Against Ecology in Jharkhand' in *This is Our Homeland: A Collection of Essays on the Betrayal of Adivasi Rights in India*. Bangalore: Equations.

Prasad, B.M. 1997. *Santal Parganas Tenancy Manual*. Patna: Malhotra Brothers.

Prasad, C.B. 1970. *Final Report on Survey and Settlement Operations in the District of Singhbhum (1958-1965)*. Patna: Government of Bihar.

Prasad, S. 1993. *Implementation of Land Reforms Legislations in Bihar* in Yugandhar and Iyer, 1993, 1993 *op. cit*. pp. 34-49.

Rao, N. 2003. *Study on Land Rights in the Santal Parganas,* The GOI-UNDP CBPPI/PRADAN Study. UK: University of East Anglia (Final Draft Mimeograph).

——— 2005. *Displacement from Land: Case of Santhal Parganas,* Economic and Political Weekly, XL, No. 41, Oct. 8-14, 2005, pp. 4439-4442.

Reid, J. 2001(1912): *Final Report on Survey and Settlement Operations in the District of Ranchi, 1902-1910* in Roy (2001), pp. 256-57.

Roy Burman, B.K. (ed). *Historical Ecology of Land Survey and Settlement in Tribal Areas and Challenges of Development (with Particular Reference to the Central Tribal Belt of India).* New Delhi: Council for Social Development.

Roy, P.R.N. 2002. *Handbook of Chotanagpur Tenancy Laws.* Allahabad: Rajpal and Company.

Roy, Pandey R.N. 2001. *Manual of Chotanagpur Tenancy Laws,* Vol. II. Allahabad: Rajpal and Company.

Roy, S.C. 1912. *Mundas and Their Country.* Calcutta.

Roy, S.C. 1937. *The Kharias.* Ranchi: Man in India Office.

Saxena, N.C. n.d. *Tenancy Reforms Vs Open Market Leasing — What Would Serve the Poor Better?* New Delhi: Planning Commission, Government of India.

Yugandhar, B.N. and Iyer, K.G. (eds.), 1993. *Land Reforms in India: Bihar Institutional Constraints.* New Delhi: Sage Publications.

Sharan, R. 2005. *Alienation and Restoration of Tribal Land in Jharkhand: Current Issues and Possible Strategies,* Economic and Political Weekly, October 8.

Sharma, K.L. 1990. *Demand for Jharkhand Genesis,* Times of India, 20 May.

Singh, K.S. 1966. *The Dust Storm and the Hanging Mist.* Calcutta.

Singh, S.K. (ed.), 2002. *A Compendium of Revenue Circulars.* Patna: Malhotra Brothers.

Thapar, R. and Siddiqi, M.H. 2003. *Chotanagpur: The Pre-Colonial and Colonial Situation,* in Ram Dayal Munda and S. Bosu Mullick (eds.) *The Jharkhand Movement: Indigenous People's Struggles for Autonomy in India.* Copenhagen: IWGIA and BIRSA, pp. 31-72.

Taylor, FEA. 2001 (1938): *Final Report of Land Survey and Settlement Operations in the District of Ranchi (1927-1935),* in Roy (2001) pp. 1137-1278.

TRI. 2003. *Survey of the Primitive Tribal Groups in Jharkhand.* Ranchi: Tribal Research Institute.

Tuckey, A.D. [2001(1920)]. *Report on the Settlement of the Kolhan Government Estate* in Roy, (1001), op. cit. pp. 647-806.

Upadhya, C. 2003. *Rights to Land In Jharkhand: Laws, Policies and Practices*, Report of Study Commissioned by GOI-UNDP under CBPPI/PRADAN Project on Pro-Poor Policies and Laws in Jharkhand. Bangalore: National Institute of Advanced Sudies (Draft Unpublished).

———2005. *Community Rights in Land in Jharkhand*, Economic and Political Weekly, XL. No. 41, Oct. 8-14. pp, 4435-4438.

Vagholikar, N., K. Moghe and R. Dutta. 2003. Undermining India—Impacts of Mining on Ecologically Sensitive Areas. Pune: Kalpavriksh.

Annexure

Last updated: 27.08.08

List of MoU signed for Mega Investment in Jharkand

S. No	*Name of the Company*	*Products*	*Capacity*	*Location*	*Project Cost (Rs. In Crore)*
1.	M/s Monnet Ispat Ltd. New Delhi	(a) Sponge Iron (b) Steel (c) Power	0.8MtPA 7 LTPA 250 MW	Hazaribag	1,400.00
2.	M/s Vallabh Steel Ltd.Ludhiana	(a) Sponge Iron (b) Pig Iron (c) Steel (d) Power	3 LTPA 1.5 Mt/A 2LTPA 40 MW	Gamharia	288.00
3.	M/s Aadhunic Alloys & Power Ltd. Jamshedpur	(a) Sponge Iron (b) Steel (c) Power (d) Pelletisation	1.98 Mt/A 2.6 Mt/yr 145 MW 2.0 Mt/yr.	Kandra	5,517.00
4.	M/s Nilanchal Iron & Power Ltd. Kolkata	(a) Sponge Iron (b) Power (c) Steel	5 LTPA 25 MW 2.0 LT/A	Chandil	250.00
5.	M/s Pawanjai Steel & Power Ltd., Lohardaga	(a) Sponge Iron (b) Steel (c) Power	2 LTPA 4 LTPA 16 MW	Lohardaga	200.00
6.	M/s Chattisgarh Electricty Co Ltd., Raipur	(a) Sponge Iron (b) Steel (c) Power	4.5 LTPA 4 LTPA 100 MW	Chaibasa	1,000.00
7.	M/s Narbhey Ram Gaspoint Pvt. Ltd. Jamshedpur	(a) Sponge Iron (b) Steel (c) Power	1.35 LTPA 0.45 LTPA 8MW	Jamshedpur	100.00
8.	M/s Jharkhand Ispat Pvt. Ltd. Hazaribag	(a) Sponge Iron (b) Steel (c) Power	10.8 LTPA 2.0 LTPA 45 MW	Ramgarh	400.00
9.	M/s Balajee Metal & Sponge Ltd.Kolkata	(a) Sponge Iron (b) Steel	1.8 LTPA 1.0 LTPA	Chaibasa	160.00
10.	M/s Abhijeet Infrastructure Pvt. Ltd., Nagpur	(a) Sponge Iron (b) Steel	2.5 LTPA 1.1 LTPA	Hazaribag	300.00

11. M/s R. G Steel Pvt.Ltd. Kolkatta	(a) Sponge Iron (b) Steel (c) Power	0.9 LTPA 0.6 LTPA 8 MW	Near Patratu	200.00
12. M/s Corporate Ispat Alloys Ltd., Kolkata	(a) Sponge Iron (b) Steel (c) Power	2.5 LTPA 1.1 LTPA	Hazaribag	300.00
13. M/s Prasad Group Ressource Pvt Ltd, Kolkata	(a) Sponge Iron (b) Steel (c) Power	1.05 LTPA 2.2 LTPA 12 MW	Near Patratu	400.00
14. M/s Horizon Eximp Ltd., Bilaspur	(a) Sponge Iron	4 LTPA	Chaibasa	74.15
15. M/s Prakash Ispat, New Delhi	Pig Iron	2 LTPA	Chaibasa	71.40
16. M/s Spectrum Mercantile Pvt. Ltd.Giridih	(a) Sponge Iron	4 LTPA	Chaibasa	74.15
17. M/s AML Steel & Power Ltd.Chennai	(a) Sponge Iron (b) Steel (c) Power	15.4 LTPA 2.0 LTPA 312 MW	Saraikela	1,944.00
18. M/sChaibasa Steel Pvt. Ltd., New Delhi	(a) Sponge Iron	4 LTPA	W.Singh-bhum	74.15
19. M/s Annpurna Global Ltd, Kolkata	(a) Sponge Iron (b) Steel (c) Power	2.01 LTPA 1 LTPA 10MW	W.Singh-bhum	500.00
20. M/s Electro Steel Integrated Ltd, Kolkata	(a) Sponge Iron (b) Steel Plant (c) Power Plant	2.0Mt/A 3.0 Mt/A 210 MW	Chandan Kyari Bokaro	8157.00
21. M/s Balajee Industrial Products Ltd. Jaipur, Rajasthan	(a) Sponge Iron	1.20 LTPA	Chaibasa	61.00
22. M/s Rungta Mines ltd. Rungta House, Chaibasa	(a) Sponge Iron (b) Power	5.1 LTPA 34 MW	Gaisuti, West Singhbhum	517.00
23. M/s Raj Refractories (P) Ltd., Ranchi	(a) Sponge Iron (b) Steel (c) Power	0.6 LTPA 0.60 LTPA 12 MW	Bundu	68.50
24. M/s Sunflag Iron &Steel Co. Ltd. 401, Chiranjiv Tower, 43, Nehru Place, New Delhi -110019	(a) Sponge Iron (b) Steel	6 LTPA 4.9 LTPA	Saraikela	937.61
25. M/s ESSAR Steel Jharkhand Ltd. (formerly M/s Hy- Grade Pellets Ltd.)	(a) Pellet Plant (b) Sponge iron (c) Steel (d) Power Plant	8.0 MtPA 7.5 MtPA 6 MtPA 2x500MW	W.Singh-bhum	9,900.00
26. M/s Anindita Trades & Investment Ltd. Vikash Bhawan , Ranchi	(a) SpongeIron (b) Power	3.34 LTPA 12 MW	Ramgarh	300.00
27. M/s BMW Industries Ltd. Park Street Kolkata	(a) Sponge Iron (b) Steel (c) Pig Iron	2.1 LT/A 0.5 MtPA 0.5Mt PA	Chandil	591.00

28. M/s Goel Sponge Pvt. Ltd. Z-262Naragaha WHS,New Delhi	(a) Sponge Iron (b) Steel (c) Power	1.15 LTPA 0.9LTPA 10 MW	W.Singh-bhum	67.00
29. M/s Hindalco Industries Ltd.	(a) Aluminium Plant (b) Captive Power Plant	3.25Lt/Yr 600 MW	Latehar (Tumbagarh)	7,800.00
30. M/s Tech Al Corporation USA	Aluminuum Plant		6,500.00	
31. M/s Jindal Steel & Power Ltd. New Delhi	(a) Pellet Plant (b) Sponge iron (c) Steel (d) Power Plant	6.0 MtPA 5.0 MtPA 5.0 Mt/PA 1000MW	Ghatshila	11,500.00
32. M/s Contisteel Ltd. New Delhi	(a) Sponge iron (b) Steel (c) Liquid steel (d) Power Plant	1.2 MtPA 1.14 MtPA 1.25 MtPA -	Chandil	1,560.00
33. M/s Kohinoor Steel Pvt. Ltd., Kolkatta	(a) Sponge iron (b) Pig Iron (c) Coal washery (d) Power Plant	2.25 LtPA 1.2LtPA 1.1 MtPA 46 MW	Buladih near Chandil	410.00
34. M/s Bhushan Power & Steel Limited	(a) Sponge iron (b) Steel (c) Power Plant	1.5 MtPA 3.0 MtPA 900 MW -	Asanboni, Jamshedpur	10,500.00
35. M/s Kalyani Steel Limited, Mundhawa, Pune	(a) Sponge iron (b) Steel (c) Power Plant	2.30 LtPA 10LtPA 80 MW	Silli, Ranchi	1,843.30
36. M/s Tata Steel Ltd, (Green Field Project)	Integrated Steel Plant	12 Mt/ year	Manohar-pur/Chandil	42,000.00
37. M/s Tata Steel Ltd, (Expansion)	Integrated Steel Plant	5 Mt/year	Jamshedpur	11,000.00
38. M/s V.S. Dempo & Company Pvt. Ltd.	Integrated Steel Plant	0.5 Mt/ year	Manoharpur	1,016.00
39. M/s Arcelor Mittal Limited	Integrated Steel Plant	12 Mt/ year		40,000.00
40. M/s JSW Steel Ltd.	Integrated Steel Plant	10 Mt/ year	Heslong, Nimdih	35,000.00
41. M/s Ranchi Integrated Steel Limited	Integrated Steel Plant	1.5 Mt/ year	Silli, Near Muri	5,452.00
42. M/s Burnpur Cement Ltd., Asansol	Cement	1 Mt/year	Patratu, Hazaribag	500.00
43. M/s Jupiter Cement Industries, Hazaribag	Cement	600TPD	Bandhuwa, Saraikela-Kharswan	90.00
44. M/s VST Tillers Tractors Limited, Bengalore	Power Tiller	8000 Nos/y	Getalsud Industrial Area, Ranchi	64.00

45.	M/s ESSEL Mining & Industries Limited, Kolkata	Integrated Steel Plant	1.75 Mt/yr Power Plant	Saraikela-Kharswan 60 MW	1,900.00
46.	M/s Sesa Goa Limited, Panji, Goa	Integrated Steel Plant	0.5 Mt/yr	Saraikela-Kharswan	1,242.00
47.	M/sMukand Steel, Bombay	Integrated Steel Plant	2.0 Mt/yr	Barlanga, Hazaribag	4,335.00
48.	M/sCement Manufacturing Company Ltd., Kolkata	Cement Plant	1.0 Mt/yr	Hazaribag Patratu,	450.00
49.	M/sFeegrade & Company Pvt. Ltd., Barbil, Orissa	Integrated Mini Steel Plant	0.3 Mt/yr	Gura & Rangamati West Singhbhum	688.80
50.	M/s Bonai Industrial Company Limited, Barbi. Orissa	Integrated Mini Steel Plant	0.25Mt/yr	Kundubera & Singh Pokharia, West Singhbhum	819.00
51.	M/s Rungta Mines ltd. Rungta House ,Chaibasa	(a) Steel (b) Power Plant	Additional 4.5 Mt/A 600 MW	Gaisuti, West Singhbhum	11,320.00
52.	M/s Rungta Mines Limited, Rungta House, Chaibasa	Cement Plant	2.5 Mt/yr	Khunta, West Singhbhum	1,312.60
53.	M/s Vini Iron & Steel Udyog Limited , Kolkata	Integrated Steel Plant	0.6 Mt/yr	Lupungdih, Chandil, Saraikela-Kharswan	880.64
54.	M/s Narsingh Ispat Limited, Howrah	Mini Steel Plant	0.25 Mt/yr	Khunti, Chandil, Saraikela-Kharswan	610.00
55.	M/s Core Steel & Power Ltd., Mumbai	Mini Steel Plant	1.00 Mt/yr	Musabani, Ghatsila, East Singhbhum	3,300.00
56.	M/s Ispat Industry Ltd., Bombay	Integrated Steel Plant	2.8 Mt/yr	Nandpur, Manoharpur, West Singhbhum	6,750.00
57.	M/s Ma Chandi Durga Ispat Ltd. Kolkata	Integrated Steel Plant Power Plant	1.1 Mt/yr 50 MW	Nala Block Jamtara District	1,500.00
58.	M/s Jagdamba Fiscal Services Ltd., Kolkaa	Integrated Steel Plant Power	1.1 Mt/Yr 50 MW	Raniswar Block, Sikaripara, Dumka	1,500.00
59.	M/s Brahmi Impex Ltd., Kolkata	Integrated Steel Plant Power	1.1 Mt/Yr 50 MW	Afjalpur, Nala Block, Jamtara	1,500.00

60.	M/s Adhunik Corporation Ltd. Kolkata	Integrated Steel Plant Power	1.1 Mt/Yr 50 MW	Kumrabad Block, Dumka	1,500.00
61.	M/s Traingle Trading Pvt. Ltd., New Delhi	Steel Plant Power	0.24 Mt/Yr 41 MW	Saraikela-Kharswan	300.00
62.	M/s Premier Ferro Alloys & Securities Ltd., Kolkata	Steel Plant	1.00 Mt/Yr	Barlanda, Ranchi	1,830.00
63.	M/s Pushp Steels & Mining (P) Ltd., Delhi	Steel Plant	0.25 Mt/Yr	Chandil	361.00
64.	M/s Sarthak Industries Ld., Mumbai	Steel Plant	2.2 Mt/Yr	Raj Kharswan	6,300.00
65.	M/s Jindal Steel & Power Ltd. (Patratu Project)	Steel Plant	6.0Mt/Yr	Patratu	18,560.00
66.	M/s Swati Udyog Pvt. Ltd.	Clinkerization Plant Cement Grinding	1000 TPD	Juri, East Singhbhum	94.50
67.	M/s Bhushan Steel Limited, International Trade Tower, Nehru Place, New Delhi- 19	Integrated Steel Plant Power Plant	3.1 Mt/yr. 300 MW	Galudih East Singhbhum	7,000.00
68.	M/s Ma Chhinmastika Sponge Iron Ltd. Jatra Tand, Kokar, Ranchi	Integrated Steel Plant Power Plant	1 Mt/yr. 60 MW	Binjhar, Ramgarah	1,840.00
69.	M/s Maa Chhinmastika Cement and Ispat Pvt. Ltd. Jatra Tand, Kokar, Ranchi	Integrated Steel Plant Power Plant	0.128 Mt/yr. 10 MW	Ramgarah	353.53
70.	M/s V.M. Salgaocar & Brothers Pvt. Ltd. Salgaocar House off Fancisco Luies Gomes Road, Post Box No. 14, Vasco-Da-Gama, Goa	Integrated Mini Steel Plant Power Plant	0.5 Mt/yr. 100 MW	Ghatshila	847.00
71.	M/s Ramgarh Sponge Iron Pvt. Ramgarh	Integrated Steel Plant	0.5 Mt/yr.	Ramgarh	785.00
72.	S.K.S. Ispat & Power Limited 50,13, Elegant Park, Andheri Kurla, Mumbai	Integrated Steel Plant	1.1 Mt/yr.	Kanchi, Ranchi	3,174.00
73.	M/s Jupiter Iron Industries Pvt. Ltd. Boddam Bazar, Hazribag	Integrated Steel Plant	0.25 Mt/yr.	Ramgarh	665.00
74.	M/s Jindal Steel and Power Ltd. Jindal Centre, 12, Bhikaji Kama Place, New Delhi- 110066	Alumina Refinary Plant	1.4 Mt/yr.	Mcluskie-gunj, Ranchi	3,350.00
		Total	**293,360.33**		

Poems

Adivasi Poem of Festivals

Oh Great Spirit of high heavens.
Mother Earth down below.
You rise like milk,
you set like curd.
Four corners, ten directions,
East, west, north, south.
The earth extending far,
the sky bending low,
spread like a mat,
covered like a bowl.
Plants and trees, animals and birds,
forests and hills, rivers and plains.
They are all your creation,
they are all your making,
they are all supported by you,
they are all protected by you.

Today, on this day of Sarhul,
today, on this day of festivity,
we, your children, we, your off-spring,
we invite you, we call upon you,
Come and sit with us, come and talk with us.
A cup of rice beer,
a plate of mixed gruel.
You drink with us, you eat with us.

The hill spirits of the hill,
the forest spirits of the forest,
the water spirits of the deep,
the *Nag, Nagin* and others
who watch our fields,
who protect our wealth,
who give success at hunt,
who dispel sickness and misery,
when afflicted with stomach ache
and head ache,
you protect us and give us peace.

The village spirits of the village,
the house spirit of the house,
our elders, our foreparents, our ancestors,
the path you made, the road you showed,
we follow after you, we emulate your example.
We invite you, we call upon you.
You sit with us, you talk with us.
A cup of rice beer,
a plate of mixed gruel.
You drink with us, you eat with us.

You who have come here,
you who have arrived here,
we sitting with you,
we seated with you,
To you gods, to you goddesses,
we offer a prayer, we make a request,
our cultivation and crops,
our animals and wealth,
may they grow day by day,
may they multiply always.
On the road we tread, on the path we walk,
let there be no threat of tigers,
let there be no fear of snakes,
let there be no splinter,

let there be no stumbling.
Jealousy among us,
anger and greed among us,
let them be uprooted, let them be destroyed.
Sickness and trouble, pain and misery,
whichever direction they may come from,
let them go back in the same direction,
let them return to the same direction.

From you gods, from you goddesses,
we expect these things,
we hope for these things.

Johar! Johar! Johar!

With Permission from:
ADI-DHARAM
Religious beliefs of the Adivasis of India
By Ram Dayal Munda
Publishers: sarini and BIRSA

Adivasi Poem of Life Cycle Rituals

In the shade of the highest god,
under the protection of Mother Earth,
This child of ours, this offspring of ours,
in our brotherhood,
in the family of our relatives,
He/she will be counted among them,
he/she will be recognized among them,
Before today, till yesterday,
He/she was counted outside of us,
he/she was considered separate from us.
From today onwards, in our groups,

in the family of our relatives,
He/she will be included,
He/she will be taken into account.
In hunger, in thirst,
in sickness, in misery,
the community will be his/her shade,
society will be his/her umbrella.

From the highest God of heaven,
From Mother Earth down below,
we make a prayer, we make a wish,
this re-accepted child,
this re-embodied offspring,
may he/she grow healthy,
may he/she grow strong,
may he/she be endowed with strength,
may he/she be endowed with wisdom
May he/she learn to socialize,
may he/she learn to work hard.
For his/her family,
for his/her country and the world,
with this child, with this young person,
may we all be healthy, may we all be well.

Sitting together through him/her,
seeing each other through him/her,
let it continue like this, let it recur like this.

Johar! Johar! Johar!

With Permission from:
ADI-DHARAM
Religious beliefs of the Adivasis of India
By Ram Dayal Munda
Publishers: sarini and BIRSA